GW00601385

New Stuff

puma.com

TX-3. AVAILABLE AT THE PUMA STORE AND SELECT RETAILERS. BUTTERFLIES NOT INCLUDED.

I have been collecting banknotes for several years. I collect in two categories (ok, three if you count trying to make a living): Test Notes and Notes That People Have Written On. In terms of their numismatic value, the main difference is that Test Notes are unused, therefore graded as Crisp Uncirculated or CU, whereas the other notes are obviously very used, hardly making it into the Very Good or VG grade.

Paul Elliman

Promotional bank note by Dutch printers Joh, Enschedé. (CU)

One Brazilian real note: 'VAI E VOLTE' ['Go and come back']. (VG)

Across the United States, and in some international locations frequented by American tourists, machines with a large crank on the front can smash what is otherwise a near-valueless one-cent coin into a site-specific "Souvenir Penny" for fifty additional cents. I have collected these smashed pennies – also called flattened, elongated, pressed, rolled, squished or souvenir pennies – for a very long time, though I lost most of the early ones, including one from the St Louis Arch that I used to jam a parking meter on a particularly bad day.

I am by no means a serious collector – particularly when compared to some – I simply like them. For those who more than like smashed pennies there are The Elongated Collectors (TEC), an association with over 2,000 members, and the Squished Penny Museum in Washington, DC, which displays over 5,000 smashed pennies in the front room of a house.

There are a number of collectors that are obsessed with history – collecting, buying and trading in order to extend their collections back through time, to get as near as possible to the first flattened pennies which made their debut at the Chicago World's Fair of 1893. There are also those interested in collecting pennies from as many places and tourist destinations as possible, and some others that simply want to collect as many as they can.

My reason for collecting is the basic appeal of cranking a penny through the gears of a strange, antiquated piece of machinery in order to receive it back no longer a coin but a bizarre copper token commemorating my visit to wherever it is that I happened to locate a "Souvenir Penny" machine. Where better to imprint a memory than on what is arguably one of the least memorable items I encounter on a daily basis… which otherwise would have ended up in a jar on my dresser or on the floor of my car.

Jennifer Gange

2

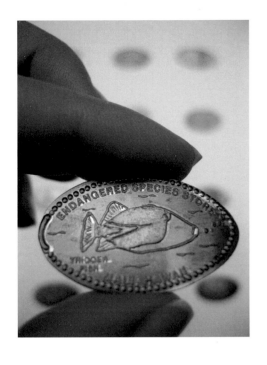

This is a drawing I made of a 5,000
Cruzeiro bill from 1985. That was the
name of Brazilian currency at the time.
Brazilians switch currencies almost
every ten years 'cause inflation is out
of control. The man on the bill is my
great grandfather. My mother's father's
father that is.

His name is Humberto Castello Branco.
He became president of Brazil in the 60s
after a military coup. He was a general
and the army pushed him forward as the
country's leader. I am not sure if he was
a puppet or really had a lot to say.

When I ask my mother about him she
always says he was an OK president.
The country was very messy and needed
a change. After him more presidents/
dictators came and things got worse
because of power games. Later Brazil
returned to democracy.

I don't think he was a very cruel and
greedy dictator because my family is not
that rich. They're not poor either.
Four years after he resigned he died
in a plane crash, and no one knows if
the accident was a political assasination
or not.

Rafael Rozendaal

Banknotes don't really have any physical value...so what makes us trust that they are worth something? Is it their visual language, or some tactile quality? Or is it simply based on our trust and belief in the society that uses them? These questions fuel my investigation into what makes a banknote more than just a rectangular piece of paper.

If with a set of devised visual codes, we can increase a piece of paper's value two-hundredfold, what happens, if we apply that same system to other objects, are we increasing their value in the same way? Can value be encoded?

In Switzerland they are using a new and unique system to create the images on their banknotes. This technique uses a redesigned halftone system, with complex customised units instead of standard dots. The result is a brain numbing level of technical and visual complexity. However, although this technique is extremely difficult to forge, it is possible to understand the way in which it works. By carefully studying the swiss banknotes I have been able to develop a system that works in a very similar way and have used this to create my own encoded images.

In this example I have encoded a traditional wallpaper designed by Willam Morris. It has been encoded with a combination of the system I developed from studying the swiss banknotes and with other variations I have developed since. The finished piece contains a watermark, micro lettering and registration techniques, but sadly these are lost in this magazine reproduction.

Whether this idea works as a value enhancing tool is a matter of debate, but as an anti-counterfeit device...it works pretty damn well.

Christopher Pearson
www.christopherpearson.com

4

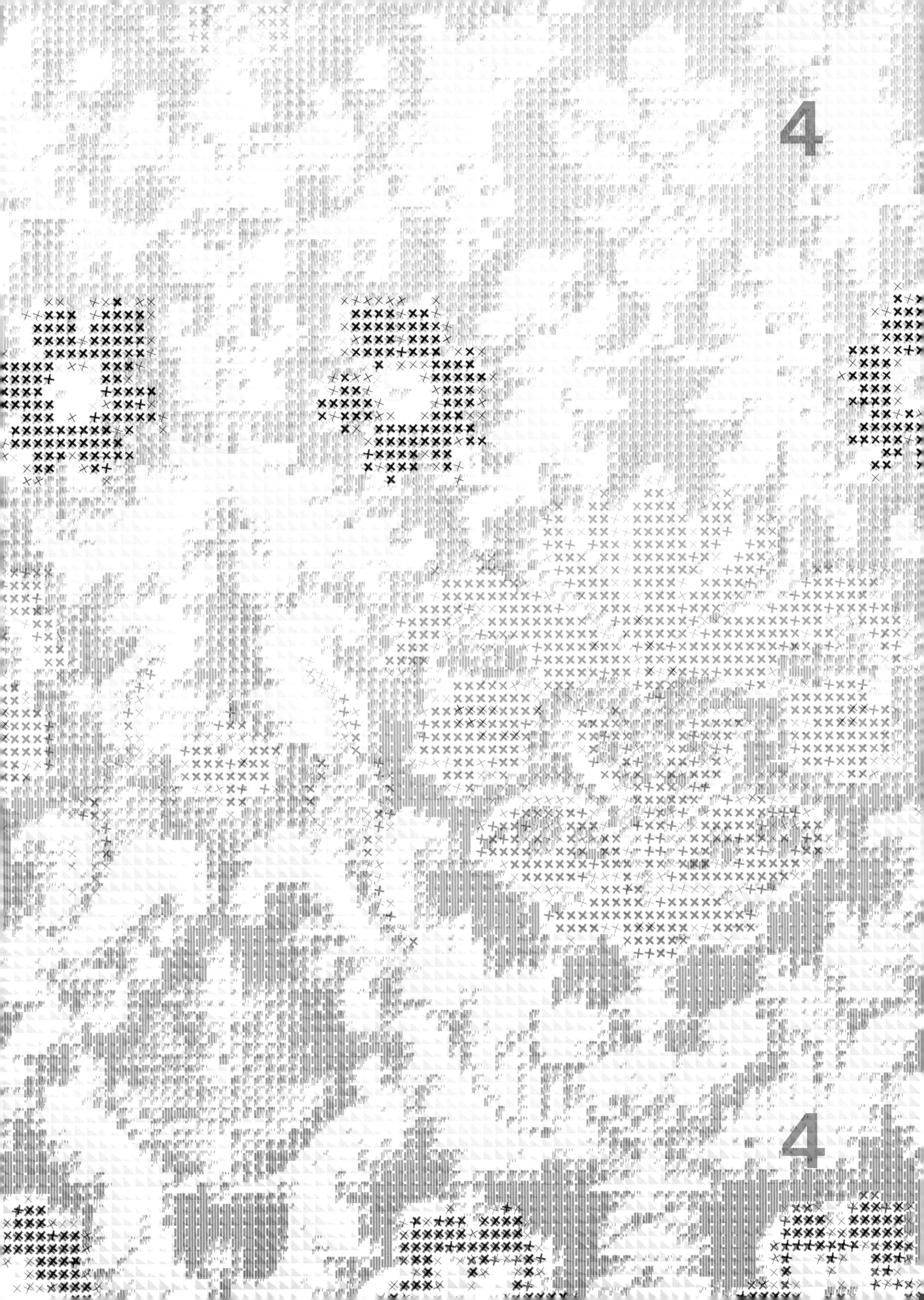
4
4

Graphic Magazine
Issue Seven

Editors
Marc-A Valli
    Editor-in-Chief
    marc@magmabooks.com
Lachlan Blackley
    Features Editor
    lachlan@magmabooks.com
Samuel Baker
Sebastian Campos
Mairi Duthie
Inca Starzinsky

Design
Samuel Baker
Sebastian Campos (Aficionado)
Inca Starzinsky

Design Assistance
Daniel Harding

Publisher
Rudolf van Wezel

Production
Rietje van Vreden

Advertising & Marketing
Mairi Duthie
T +44 7780 707 004

Printing
Drukkerij Tuijtel
Hardinxveld-Giessendam
The Netherlands

Paper
For this edition the paper choice has been selected
from the international assortment of Schneider
Papier Benelux. For more information please visit
www.schneider-papier.nl

Luxocard I, 250gsm
by Cartiere Burgo
[one-sided SBS-Board]
    Cover
Luxo Pak Silk, 150gsm
by Stora Enso
[practically woodfree silk coated art paper]
    pp1–64,129–144
Luxo Magic, 150gsm
by Stora Enso
[woodfree gloss coated art paper]
    pp65–112
Planospeed, 120gsm, volume 1.32
[woodfree offset paper,
made from Eucalyptus fibres]
    pp113–128
Recystar, 150 gsm, volume 1.30
by Lenzing
[high bulk uncoated paper,
made from 100% recycled fibres]
    pp145–176

Addresses

Editorial
Graphic Magazine
c/o Magma
117–119 Clerkenwell Road
London, EC1R 5BY
United Kingdom
T +44 20 7242 9522
F +44 20 7242 9504
graphic@magmabooks.com
www.magmabooks.com

**Publishing, Subscriptions
and Advertising**
BIS Publishers
Herengracht 370–372
NL-1016 CH Amsterdam
The Netherlands
T +31 20 524 75 60
F +31 20 524 75 57
graphic@bispublishers.nl
www.bispublishers.nl

Subscription rates
(all prices include airmail)

1 year (4 issues)
    Europe: EUR80/£55
    USA/Canada: US$105
    Other countries: US$125

2 years (8 issues)
    Europe: EUR149/£103
    USA/Canada: US$195
    Other countries: US$225

Student subscription
(valid only with a copy of your
student registration form)

1 year (4 issues)
    Europe: EUR63/£43.50
    USA/Canada: US$90
    Other countries: US$100

How to subscribe?
Use the subscription card in the magazine or
mail, fax or e-mail us your name, company name,
(delivery) address, country & telephone/fax
number and the type of subscription you require.
Please include details of your credit card type,
number, expiry date and your signature. If paying by
Mastercard, please also add the CVC-2 code (last
3 digits of the number printed on the signature strip
of the credit card). If the delivery address is not the
same as the credit card's billing address please also
state the billing address. If you do not wish to pay by
credit card please mention that you wish to receive
an invoice. Your subscription will start after payment
is received.

A BIS Publishers Publication

All rights reserved. No part of this publication may
be reproduced or transmitted in any form or by
any means, electronic or mechanical, including
photocopy, recording or any information storage and
retrieval system, without permission in writing from
the copyright owner(s).

The utmost care has been taken to present the
information in Graphic as accurately as possible.
For any damage that may result from use of that
information neither the publisher nor the authors can
be held responsible. All efforts have been made to
contact copyright holders. Questions can be directed
to: Graphic, Amsterdam, the Netherlands.

ISSN 1569-4119
ISBN 90-6369-092-4

Copyright © 2005
BIS Publishers
Amsterdam, The Netherlands

BIS PUBLISHERS

Editorial
Green hills of Lake Geneva

By Marc-A Valli

I. Scene by the lake.

If you ever visit Lake Geneva you will not fail to
notice the beauty of the landscapes that surround it.
At the end of the summer the vineyards slide down steep
hills in cascades of grapes, interrupted only by a few
manor houses and footpaths and rocks. When you walk
through these hills with the lake at your feet you do
not feel that you are looking at something preserved,
something old or ancient, but rather at something
ageless, timeless.

This landscape, however, is not there by accident.
It is there because of the efforts of pioneering
environmental activist Franz Weber to foster a law
protecting the Lavaux and its hills in the sixties.
Without that law we would now be looking at a more built-
up replica of the Costa Del Sol. But not all locals were
pleased with Franz Weber's efforts. Landowners and real
estate developers felt cheated. There would have been an
extraordinary amount of money to be made by selling that
view — well, while it lasted.

Franz Weber and local real estate owners and
developers saw things differently and this brings me to
the subject of this piece: how do we give value to things.
What's worth more, for instance in this case, is it the
beauty of an unspoilt landscape or the real estate value
of that same land? Are we looking for long or short-term
investment? It's not always easy making money out of
something that is ageless, timeless — and priceless.

II. The Barbarians.

The various peoples, the Helvetians, the Alamans,
the Burgundians, the Lombards, the Franks and all the
other so-called Barbarians who occupied that region
before, during, and then again after the Roman empire
didn't know a lot about money. The first societies were
based on barter, on the direct exchange of goods, as in,
'You give you me a slave and I'll give you half a dozen jars
of wine,' or 'You plough my field and I'll give you a sack of
wheat,' or 'You fight wars on my side and I promise to give
you a title and a chunk of my land.'

And in and around this bartering process rapports
of power and systems of value evolved. But far from being
a utopia, this primitive mode of commerce could be highly
traumatic. It would breed instability, resentment. It
would promote a feeling of injustice. It was extremely
difficult for anyone to get a fair deal. Maybe you thought
that your cow was worth more than the other fellow's cart
— but how could you prove that? Breaking point was always
just down the line. A lord might not have been very happy
to carve up his domain each time he had to reward a loyal

THIS ISSUE'S UNECESSARY FACTS & FIGURES
CROWDING THE BOTTOM MARGIN:

warrior. Within this restrictive logic a deal would often degenerate into blackmailing, bullying and violence. Antediluvian grief.

III. The Utopia.
It was in order to solve such problems that we brought money into the equation. Make no mistake, money was a great invention. Money was the solution. Here you had an impartial, neutral way of measuring value. It facilitated exchange in all areas, between fields that would otherwise not have much in common. It was a way of creating order and stability. Yes, I know it seems hard to believe this today, but at that point money was a way of promoting fairness and equality (the money would still be worth the same no matter who you were or what position you occupied in the social hierarchy). In fact it was money and not barter that was the utopia.

In Switzerland this newfound harmony was particularly poignant. Banks sprouted like mushrooms in the woods and the hills around the lakes. Watchmakers adorned their works with gold and diamonds, the trains arrived on time and everyone went on skiing holidays and ate milk chocolates.

IV. Dreams come true.
But then something happened to money. Money was such a good thing it never stopped growing in terms of importance, until one day, money became the main thing. Money was the business … Money started to take itself seriously. Money would even assume a moral dimension. This new morality dictated that something that made money was good and should be allowed to live on, while something that didn't make money was bad and should be purged. Currency stopped being just a measuring device and started to call the shots. Suddenly money was capable of creating anything, of making anything happen. It changed the world. It created a new world. Money had become a god.

And not surprisingly money lost touch with reality, with its old measuring soberness. The money god fell in love with its own corrupt and inebriated imagination, with its dreams. And consequently, a new system of values came into being. A system based on just that: the dreams that money dreams, a succession of sometimes peaceful and sometimes turbulent dreams.

Take Wall Street for example, that great factory of dreams. Remember the Dotcom bubble? How something that was worth nothing suddenly became worth millions before going back to being worth nothing again in the space of a few months? How we dreamt up a market and when we woke up thousands lost their jobs?

V. El Camino de Las Vegas.
In the past pilgrims made their way to the Vatican or to Santiago de Compostela or to Canterbury Cathedral. Today, Las Vegas is the most popular tourist destination in the world. What does that tell us about our world? About the values we hold most dear?

When I talk to friends in the UK I am always shocked when I realise that they (and my friends are not City speculators) no longer buy property to settle down, to start a family, to have a roof over their heads — but as an investment. With our investments and our portfolios of shares we have all been reduced to the level of gamblers in a casino.

Las Vegas is not an accident. Las Vegas is the future model we are heading towards. Super casinos appearing like mirages in the middle of a desert, virtual worlds, worlds in which history has been replaced by theme-parks and populated not by citizens but by tourists, punters, 'suckers', 'whales', dealers and whores — dreamers, all of them. People who have gambled away the past, the present, and who are now in the process of throwing the future in. Our financial institutions, our governments, our pension schemes … — have all turned into lotteries in which the stakes keep getting higher. We know it's time to call it a day, but like a gambler caught in his own madness we cannot bring ourselves to do it. We keep playing. We keep losing. We're filled with self-loathing and self-pity, but we keep playing nevertheless. And we keep losing. The house always wins. Even when it's the house itself you're betting.

VI. By the shore of Lake Geneva.
I remember how on that late summer afternoon by the shore of Lake Geneva, instead of walking through a life-sized version of a real-estate agent's brochure (a developer's dream, an architect's dream …), I was able to find a patch of green and dream of how my ancestors hunted and brawled and partied over those then still unspoilt hills.

*   *   *

This issue's cover image is based on an illustration by Nawel [pp72–79]

11

Graphic
Magazine
Issue
Seven:
Money

Look
+ Read
+ Use

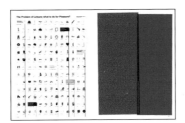

IMAGE SOURCE

Image Source Triple Disc Offer.
Buy three Image Source discs for £499.*

During February and March 2005, you can buy three Image Source
discs for just £499. Simply pick any three discs from a list of 100 titles
available at www.imagesource.com. It's our best offer yet!

SATISF

*Terms and conditions apply.

Further rewards for your purchases.
Register for the new Image Source WISH scheme.

With the WISH scheme you'll earn WISHES for every purchase you make
which you can then redeem for gift vouchers throughout the year.
For details visit www.imagesource.com/wish or call +44 (0) 20 7075 1111.

ACTION

The story, as art historians will tell it, will be about work that didn't fit where it was supposed to. It will be about a different kind of gallery space where that same work found a home. It will be a story full of dedicated hosts, unusual guests, late nights and, of course, multiple beer runs.

Riviera Gallery

Interview by Sebastian Campos

About two years ago five people decide to open a new gallery in Brooklyn, NY…How did this come about? Did New York really need a new gallery? John Hobbs: We collectively were surrounded by a bunch of talented/interesting people who in turn knew a lot of other talented/interesting people. And we thought it would be fun to give this diverse lot a loose, open-minded venue that wasn't as strictly business-minded as some of the other places in New York. For the neighborhood, we got the place relatively cheap so we knew we wouldn't be under pressure financially to book only shows that were likely to sell. *John Tymkiw:* We were all looking for a place where we could do what we wanted with no restrictions, and we all like art and like to party. *Matt Campbell:* I don't know if New York needs anymore galleries in general, but I guess we felt there weren't any that were consistently showing this kind of work, that were nice and relaxed and with fun openings. Many seem too serious for their own good or just have bad art. Since around the time we opened, a few more have opened up with a similar vibe — the Stay Gold Gallery for instance. *Matt Owens:* I had a show idea, and had all of the artists ready to go. And I could not find a venue that I felt made sense for the kind of work I wanted to

show. So, when Matt Campbell and the rest of the guys decided to start a gallery I became a partner. Because we all are involved in the same culture of art and design, I think it just sort of made sense and felt right. *Bill Moulton:* It never felt as though we were setting out to open a gallery in the traditional sense. We all just wanted a venue to bring together our common interests in art and design, as well as our different angles on them. Almost like a community center for 'our' community of artists. And from there, it just grew organically into what it is. New York does not necessarily need another new gallery…but there's always room for a new kind of gallery.

What was your first show? JH: The first show was pretty hot; it was called 'Fugitives' for the outlaw street level nature of many of the artists. The show included the likes of Travis Millard, Lee Misenheimer, Scien & Klor, Niko Stumpo, Matt Owens and Rick Froberg from the Hot. *MC:* Yeah, it was absolutely freezing outside, and this huge amount of people packed into the space — and they stayed there until we finally threw them out at about 1am. We did multiple beer runs — at one point it was so packed we couldn't load the beer in — couldn't get the handtruck into the space, so we had to pass it over people's heads. It certainly started with a bang. *MO:* It was amazing to have had this idea, and to go through the whole process of converting the storefront into a functioning gallery, getting the artists together, and then have a ton of people show up in the freezing cold. It blew me away. *BM:* I really enjoyed that whole process of transformation, as it truly reaffirmed my belief that you can make anything out of anything. The whole thing felt like a design project.

Above
Opening night for **Fugitives**

Top right
Paul Clark

Right
Matt Owens

Below
Lee Mishenheimer

'It never felt as though we were setting out to open a gallery in the traditional sense.'

'Art should be affordable, and you should be able to get some and take it home if you really like it.'

Top
Trespassers Will Be Eaten

Above
The Free Library

Right
Amalgomolm

Did you have a 'masterplan'? Was there a 'gallery agenda' that connected the shows to one another? JH: As far as a masterplan goes, we just wanted the whole experience to be somewhat loose and fun. That doesn't mean we didn't put a lot of work/labor into it. It just means that the gallery isn't about commerce; it's about showing compelling work, and having a few drinks with friends, meeting interesting people. The only thread that ties the shows together is that they have been embraced by the five of us, which has led down many diverse avenues. JT: We try to keep it pure — that is — interesting to us. It's our collective selfish pleasure, and everyone's invited to have a look. MO: I think we have refined our ideas of what the gallery should be over the past two years. You put on shows that do well, and you learn what does and does not work in the space. Also, I think meeting people like Jordan Isip and other people involved in our creative world has helped us link up with like minded individuals. Like any collective endeavour, the gallery sort of has a life of its own. As partners, we try to keep our ear to the ground, and find artists that make sense and add to the body of work.

Is there one now? JT: World domination. MC: I think the masterplan is to keep doing what we're doing and try not to screw it up by becoming too serious or worried about money. We are trying to steadily upgrade though, better lights, online store, improved website, more organization and stuff when dealing with artists and the public. I don't think there is so much a masterplan, but more a desire for steady growth/progress, etc. Ultimately, we would it like it to gather enough momentum so that it gets where it's kind of running and paying for itself. MO: There is more of a master plan now than in the past. I think we all agree on the

larger vision of what the gallery needs to foster and support. It's not a garage sale or a clubhouse. So, I think we have grown into the understanding that the shows we put on can be important for us and for the artists, and that there is the potential to do really amazing things. BM: I think masterplans are overrated. When you have five people trying to mandate a 'masterplan' things are likely to lose focus. I value the fact that we all have a slightly different take on what the space is and where it's going. And in a way, the nature of that relationship keeps things honest and fresh. In my mind, the focus lies somewhere in the fact that nothing is of one singular vision.

How was the project received by the 'mainstream' art world in NY? JH: Not sure, but I would hope that Riviera is a bit less predictable or strategic than the mainstream New York gallery system. JT: I don't really know much about the 'mainstream' art world, and they probably don't know much about us. We're about art that is accessible, to us, to most people. The 'mainstream' art world seems to be about some other world that we don't live in. We had some press about how we were a gallery in New York for 'affordable' art. Art should be affordable, and you should be able to get some and take it home if you really like it. The second show we put on, Amalgomolm, was scheduled for the night of the Williamsburg gallery crawl in honor of the Armory Show in Manhattan. We had no idea it was an event night. Many people of the art cognoscenti came by, and seemed very impressed by the g-string clad men and women dancing in our storefront. We thought it was hilarious. Dancers, video, heavy metal music, red lights, taxi drivers stopping, watching. They seemed to take it very seriously. We laughed. I guess that 's the difference between the mainstream and us. This is fun for us. This is business for them. MC: I know some of our shows have been attended by curators and directors of mainstream galleries — the MOMA and the New Museum definitely. There is one guy from the MOMA — who comes to our shows a lot. I got talking to him recently, and he was raving: 'Oh, I love this place! I keep coming back, and you know what? Sooner or

later I'm gonna like something.' — whatever that means. MO: We have had a lot of folks from the city and the more mainstream art world come in, and I know that this people know what we are doing and kind of what we are about. By our own choosing, we are trying to do things in our own way and on our own terms. For good or bad I think we are more a gallery for artists and designers first and not really an 'art collector's' gallery. BM: Word, word.

And what about the art press? JH: Funny that, we have been garnering a bit of press, but the range of publications has been pretty broad, which I think is great. We've been written up by Women's Wear Daily, Anthem, Creative Review, Citizen K, Juxtapoz, 718 New Style and now Graphic. Not quite the traditional art press which perhaps is a healthy thing, or maybe we're just making excuses. JT: Art press - we got some press, but it's from magazines we might read. That's nice. MC: I feel like there is no real official art scene any more anyway (or there is, but lots of young people are not really engaged with it. It's mostly for dealers and extremely wealthy people). There is the established press, who kind of mostly cover museums and dealer galleries, but the scene itself has fragmented so much — and there's so much other stuff going on — on all sorts of levels. It's like what happened to the popular music scene around the seventies or so. It used to be one style dominated at a time, and now it's all over the place with Rock, Pop, Rap, Punk, etc…all coexisting simultaneously. Art is the same. All sorts of things are going on simultaneously, and we're just part of the mix. And the web plays into it too, sites like Idanda (who've featured us) are covering such a wide range, from fine art to graphics, fashion design and music — and everything in between — and they have a big audience. MO: We get plenty of press given whom we are catering to. If the attendance at the openings and the sales are any indication, I think we are doing pretty well. BM: It's a great feeling when you see people taking notice of what you are doing. Especially when it comes from all angles as it has. All of a sudden, you realize that the space is reaching all sorts of people, and not just one select group.

And the Public? JH: The public seems to be very much into the Riviera dynamic, the Brooklyn Police, not so much though… *MC:* They [Brooklyn Police] loved the dancing girls in Amalgomolm though, came round asking when we're gonna do it again. They were really disappointed to find out it was art, they thought we were a strip club I think. *JT:* Every show we've had has had a great reception. When we're happy with what we're doing, people respond positively. *MO:* I think the public and the folks that go to the shows are into it. When we have an opening people can always expect a cool crowd that is neither totally pretentious people nor a bunch of skater kids being rowdy. It's more like pretentious people and skater kids drinking beer together and talking about art. *BM:* I would also say that the elderly and infants have also made appearances at our openings. So, you might say that we have the power to bring families together or destroy them, with the potent mix of art and alcohol.

How did you see the gallery's relationship with the more established spaces in New York? JH: We're surprisingly unrelated or connected to the New York gallery scene, but we have built some relationships with galleries in other places. *MC:* Ideally, I think we'd like to establish relationships with like-minded galleries around the States and the rest of the world, so that we can swap and tour shows, etc. We're just kind of letting this evolve naturally though, rather than really pushing it as an agenda — all in good time. *JT:* Don't spend much time on that. Maybe we should invite them to some shows. *MO:* As a gallery we are a baby. If we keep it going for a few years and become more established, I think we have the potential to become more part of the establishment. Part of me feels like to get there we would have to put a lot more energy into things that we don't want to do (bigger shows, more money). It's sort of, like when a band signs to a major, they lose that something that made them special. I don't think we want to lose that…not just yet. *BM:* The gallery is kind of like a beautiful adolescent girl, and we are the protective father who doesn't want her dating yet, or at any time for that matter. A good girl stays at home and loves her family…she's not out prancing the streets like some cheap strumpet.

Has this changed over time? JH: We have become more visible, but we prefer the relationships that we've always had. *MO:* I think it's too soon to tell. *BM:* Everything changes as it develops. But I think there is always a sense of what feels right, and what is just trying to be something you're not.

Is there a show you wish you'd never been involved with in the first place? JH: We're not afraid to fuck up, take a chance on something that perhaps doesn't go well, but I personally haven't been let down…yet. *MC:* I've learned that you've got to be a bit careful about what you're getting into as much as possible. I wanna see at least half a dozen pieces from the intended show before I agree to do it now, 'cos we've had experiences whereby artists change their mind and produce something very different from what was discussed, and that just creates more work, stress and unreliable results. But, regrets? No — it's a living thing. *MO:* I don't have any regrets. I think we have had shows that were not planned well or fell flat, but I think that is part of learning what to do and not to do. *BM:* I agree. Some shows do better than others, but it's better to try new things than to just curate safe shows all the time.

Is there a kind of work that you would never show? JH: We would never show those Damien Hirst fishtank pieces because maybe they would leak causing considerable water damage, and leave the place smelling poorly. Some people might try pouring beer into the tank, and I believe a couple of those had some actual live fish in them, which could be a problem with drunk fish and what not, which could in turn lead to litigation. *JT:* Boring, irritating work. Boring or irritating to us that is. *MO:* I think most work we would never show. We may show one artist out of several hundred that we get work from. It depends. It has to be the right time, right work, and right context for the show. There are a lot of variables that determine what is appropriate. In the end, I think we all just go with our gut instincts.

Which show do you think best represents the 'spirit' of the gallery? JH: Fugitives. *JT:* Yeah, Fugitives, and the last ones, Pressure Lines, Spinning Yarns and Frequent Fliers. *MO:* Fugitives, Pressure Lines, Spinning Yarn, The Free Library and Frequent Fliers. *MC:* Well, as long as everyone's voting for their own shows I think GreedyGasGuzzlers was amazing, and Trespassers Will Be Eaten. Also, Bill's show, Amalgomolm, was a highlight for me too, just because it was so out there and unexpected — and definitely very original. I think keeping the spirit of the gallery on track is important, and the quality control is key, but I'd hate to see us fall too much into a set style of work, because then it may become a little boring or predictable. *BM:* I think they all do as a whole. The broad spectrum of shows and artists is what establishes the spirit for me.

What's Riviera's 'dreamshow'? JH: Jenny Saville with Tom Sachs, Barry Mcgee, Evan Hecox and the Cro-mags. *JT:* Yeah, what you said, plus Toshio Iwai doing the lighting. *MO:* A Rich Jacobs solo show…I am going to ask him later in the week. *BM:* Mumenshantz.

How does the gallery manage to survive? JH: We actually got the space pretty cheap, put in a lot of work ourselves, and we split the rent 5 ways, plus we do sell work…sometimes. *JT:* Contributions from members. We also accept donations. *MC:* We all pitch in every month for expenses and offset costs from art sales. It's a pretty simple set up. *BM:* Communism.

'We're not afraid to fuck up, to take a chance on something that perhaps doesn't go well ...'

Above
Andrew Pommier

Top right
Neil O'Brien

Left & right
Matt Campbell
GreedyGasGuzzlers

Left
Charles Wilkens

Bottom left
Jeremy Fish

Below
Ryan Sanchez

'… people prefer
experiencing artwork
and collecting it
in a less pretentious,
intimidating
atmosphere …'

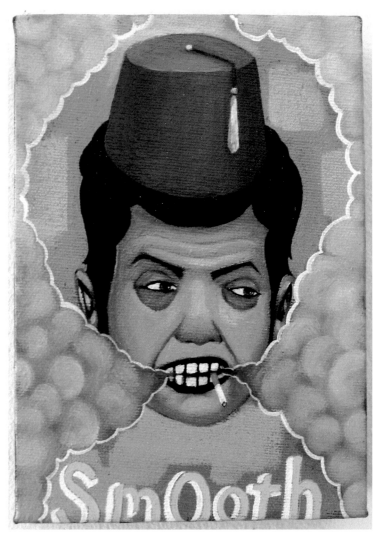

Does the reality of running an art space match up with your expectations? JH: It's really been great, well worth the effort. There are 5 of us so the burden is minimal — never really, feels like work. *JT*: We didn't really have a defined plan, so there weren't many expectations, except to have fun and show art we like. We're running our own personal art project with parties, and each show is still a new and different experience, so it's exceeded expectations in that it's still fresh. *MC*: Sometimes it feels a bit like work. Because putting on a show can take quite a bit off effort, but it's the kind of work I love to do, personally. *MO*: There have been times when I felt like it was too much work for the result, but over the last few months I realized once you focus on making something that has its own energy and direction, the gallery can really have a life of its own, and have an impact on people and on how they feel about art and art making.

Is Riviera alone? Are there other spaces (locally, nationally, internationally) you feel are operating from similar coordinates? JH: 222 in Philadelphia, and I think also Rudy's in LA. *MO*: 222, Space 1026 also in Philadelphia, The Houston Gallery (RIP) in Seattle, Art Prostitute Gallery in Texas, Camp Fig in Austin. *MC*: The Compound Gallery in Portland is another one.

Is there a 'new' art world emerging in response to new ways of making/experiencing/collecting work? JH: Hope so, I think people prefer experiencing artwork and collecting it in a less pretentious/intimidating atmosphere, and perhaps they like the idea of supporting artists — and maybe even the space — on a more local level.

MO: I think the 'new' art world is emerging as we speak. I am sure there are a handful of people we have shown that will go on to be very important in the larger art cannon. The collision of high and low art, street art, commerce and graphic design is turning art making upside down. We have artists now that have their own sneakers…it's crazy. *MC*: It's fantastic though (the sneakers). I agree that a new scene is emerging/unfolding. I like that people from different backgrounds are making art, and the whole collision thing Matt's talking about, and that making art it's not just about people who went to art school to be fine artists. I don't mean to diss them (fine artists) at all, but I find a lot of this other work more interesting right now. *BM*: Yeah, there is a whole attitude of making things more accessible by taking them over. It seems like the generation of DIY kids who started their own record labels, film companies and fashion lines in the last two decades is now doing the same thing in the art world. If the art world is inaccessible, we'll just make our own. Instead of buying products, artists are making them or redesigning them…making them their own. And the process of marketing these ideas has become as integral to artistic expression as the piece itself. While the concept of redefining art is nothing new, there is definitely a new approach emerging now.

I heard a book documenting the first year of the gallery is in the making… JH: Keep your fingers crossed on this one; we may have a book coming out from the amazing, fantastic people at Die Gestalten Verlag. *MC*: Indeed. Fingers crossed on both hands. It's gonna be more about the artists, with the gallery as the common thread. We have a work-in-progress at the gallery. It'll happen one way or another. *MO*: The book is basically done, but I think we might want to add year two in there as well.

Any other plans for the future? JH: Hopefully a big show in 2005, at Parco in Japan. *JT*: Maybe a shop. We've had several shows organized by guest curators: Ryan Sanchez, Jordan Isip. We hope to get more guest curators for shows in 2005. Moving beyond our own limited sense,

and reaching out through people who share our vision of art. *MC*: If not through Parco, I still wanna tackle Japan somehow. We have friends involved with other galleries there too. Both John T and myself used to live in Tokyo, and I think what we're doing would go down very well over there. *MO*: Better shows, maybe a store, the Japan show is possibly happening, only time will tell.

If you could rewind a couple of years, and start over knowing what you know now…would you do it all again? JH: Hell yeah! *JT*: Yep. *MC*: Do it all again for sure, but with better lighting. *MO*: I would change a few things, but I would definitely still have done it. Its something I never thought I would do in my life, so for me it's been an amazing experience, and I feel lucky to have been in the right place at the right time to make it happen. *BM*: Most definitely.

What would you do differently? JH: Would buy more beer up front so we weren't always running out trying to get more during the show, oh, and an air conditioner, a big one, and more paper towels, also would have bought that ROTGUT piece before that other guy got it. *JT*: Win the lottery. *MC*: Drink less at the openings — there's something about a continuous supply of free beer that requires concentrated restraint if you're trying to keep it together to still operate the credit card machine later on in the evening. *MO*: I think I would have tried to keep it open more days in the week. *BM*: Better heating system in the back room, and a bigger sink.

* * *

www.seeyouattheriviera.com
www.destroyrockcity.com.
www.fudgefactorycomics.com
www.abnormalbehaviorchild.com
www.volumeone.com
www.blixie.com
www.123klan.com
www.ihatephotography.com
www.indexa.com
www.greedygasguzzlers.com
www.takako.us
www.thebrm.com
www.huntergatherer.net
www.enginesystem.com
www.daveshoemakertattoos.com
greedgoblin.com/swigg

Bits and Bobs
and a few ideas for
china … Using memories
and traditional craft
techniques passed
down from her grand-
mother, Hanna Melin
explores various
materials with her
illustration. Something
old and something new.

Hanna Melin

Interview by Lachlan Blackley

Tell us a little about yourself. I was born in Sweden 1978 and my favourite thing was to play library. When I was five, my grandmother and I had meetings once a week where we did cross-stitching. I moved to Maidstone in England to do foundation studies at Kent Institute of Art and Design. After that I went to Brighton to study illustration. I moved back to Sweden after graduating and spent a year doing graphic design for a company that sold fertilizer. I didn't think that was my calling in life, and went on to do Communication Art and Design at the Royal College of Art in London. I have just graduated and am now a freelance communicator.

So what's your work about? What excites you? What excites me is to go to John Lewis haberdashery department. I love to look at the fabrics and threads. I love things that makes me smile, either a pink Hello Kitty purse or an old photograph of my grandmother in a bikini. I love to draw from books, and make the photographer's image my image. A lot of my work comes from my family and memories, the mood I am in. I like my illustrations to become something more than an image, to make them into explorations of materials as well. Like when the hard meets the soft, as in the plates, the embroidery with the china.

Can you tell us more about your work with fabric? What is the memory chair about? The chairs are about my grandmother and grandfather. They both had Alzheimer's. I decided to write down everything I remembered of what they told me about their lives, about what their mum and dad did, etc. I realised that their lives did not even fill an A4. Then I embroidered their story and drew from my grandmother's photo album, and from those images made the upholstery. I think I work a lot from fabric because it reminds me of my grandmother and my home. I like the feeling and texture the fabric can give to an image. Since I do my work on the computer I like to use things that my grandmother taught me, like the cross-stitching, it's a way of bringing traditions on in a modern way.

Your plates are really cool. What's the story behind this? My plates for 'A Kestrel For a Knave' by Barry Hines are a series of nine different designs. At the moment I am trying to find someone that will manufacture them for me. The idea was based around the book, being set in the 70s and up north, where I imagined that's what kind of decorations they would have on the wall.

What would you most like to explore or develop in the future? At the moment I am trying to put a book together, where I would like to combine all different kinds of materials into printed form. I would also like to continue exploring the transfers onto china, maybe make a whole service.

What's your Utopia? My dream is to never get stuck in a job where all I do is wait for Friday. I want to spend my life living every day, and I guess the only way you can do that is to do your dream. I just hope my dream never gets boring for me, that I will keep finding inspiration. And save the earth.

* * *

hannamelin@yahoo.co.uk
www.hannamelin.com

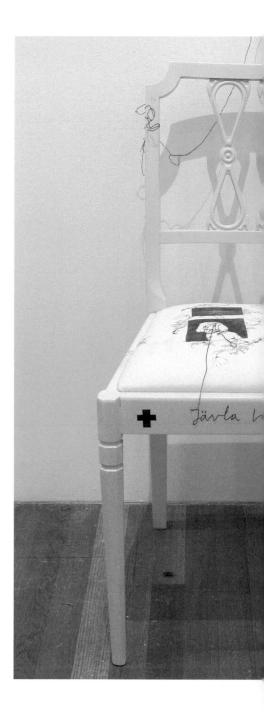

Far left
Hanna Melin
Memory Chair

Left & above left
Hanna Melin
From a series of images designed onto dinner plates, based on the book 'A Kestrel For a Knave' by Barry Hines

Page 26
Hanna Melin
Fuck You

Page 27
Hanna Melin
Top Ten Of English Words I Don't Like

Page 28
Hanna Melin
Illustration for a dinner plate, based on the book 'A Kestrel For a Knave' by Barry Hines

Page 29
Hanna Melin
English things

Issue Seven—Graphic Magazine
Show+Tell+Profile

TOP-TEN OF ENGLISH WORDS I DON'T LIKE

1. BITS AND BOBS
2. CUDDLE
3. DIN-DINS

4. INNIT
5. CHEERS (USED AS THANKYOU)

6 BLOWER
7 HOODIES
8 HOOK UP
9 CRIMBO
10 EQUILIBRIUM

I AM THINGS THAT MAKE... THE WORLD...
AFRAID ...OYING THE WORLD... ...STREET...
...ELLO GORGEOUS ON THE ...
...GIRL S/BO... ...AUSE YOU ARE A WOMAN AND A...
...LETR... ...RE... I LIVE IN BETHNAL GREEN

For Kiyoshi Kuroda there is a beautiful simplicity in animals and flowers. Working largely in black and white, his images now find their way onto fabric in a collaboration with designer Hisashi Narita.

Kiyoshi Kuroda

Interview by Lachlan Blackley

What's behind your visual aesthetic? Naturally, I think my sense of beauty is deeply influenced by the environment in which I live. Specifically, as a Japanese person, born and raised in Tokyo. To me, the aesthetic sense nurtured in this cultural environment is very important and something I value in my artistic expressions. I am often inspired by the scenery, colours and plants I see with my own eyes, as well as those in photos or books.

You appear to have a fascination with the animal and organic. Where does this come from? Since I was a little child, I have often been glued to pictorial books of animals and plants. In the beginning I think I was simply attracted to their interesting structure and beauty. Then, since I started creating my own works, I have become more fascinated by the contrasting elements co-existing in beautiful animals and flowers, such as beauty and the feeling of violence and malice (for example: the thorns of roses or mysterious patterns). My work expresses and emphasises such seemingly contradictory elements.

You've done some beautiful fabric work with Hisashi Narita. Can you tell us a little about this collaboration? I am personally very interested in fabric works. Mr Hisashi Narita, a friend of mine, is a costume designer whose works are quite original and freshly attractive. I have been trying to work out a way to collaborate with him and this was realised with the Plus+ exhibition. I paid special attention to the process of our collaboration — taking turns in creating fabric, clothes and photos.

You primarily use black and white in your most recent work. Can you tell us more about this? In 2003, when I had my exhibition in Rocket, I started creating works with a black and white world view, so to speak. With this exhibition, I try to simplify my artwork, eliminating or minimizing colours and other superfluous information, in order to emphasize the line drawing.

What are your plans for 2005? Anything new you'd like to explore? I intend to continue exploring new ways of expression and presentation as I have a strong desire to create and see my work not only in two-dimensional artworks but also in other forms such as video/film images and clothes. I am planning to hold an exhibition overseas in 2005. I hope to present my work to a larger part of the world instead of being content with working only in Japan.

*   *   *

www.kiyoshikuroda.jp

Issue Seven—Graphic Magazine
Show+Tell+Profile

Issue Seven—Graphic Magazine
Show+Tell+Profile

0.6 DOZENS OF PINK ROSES
IN TOKYO

Issue Seven—Graphic Magazine
Show+Tell+Profile

0.6 DOZENS OF WHITE ROSES
IN TOKYO

Whilst some design-ers thrive on theoretical and imaginary worlds, others are motivated by an urge to make, pro-duce (and often, sell) objects and to see their creations in every-day use.

Magic realism

Text by Mairi Duthie

Tom Dixon exemplifies the particular mixture of imagination and drive that is needed to get things 'out there'. He has a keen awareness of the business side of furniture retail, informed both by his work as creative director of Habitat and his own personal forays into furniture production and actually running his own shop (Space) in the 1990's.

His working life is based firmly in retail and commerce, and the practicalities of sales and marketing. At the same time, as the leader of creative teams both at Habitat and at his own design company Dixon has to 'make sure that flair and innovation are a key part of the design process and of our thinking. New ideas add value to whatever we are producing.'

Talking about his role in Habitat, and their recent smash hit launch of the VIP range (Very Important Product) using celebrities to design 20 objects from Monolo Blahnik's shoehorn to Ewan McGregor's director's chair, Dixon says 'We were struggling to find a hook on which to hang the 40th Birthday celebration. As Habitat itself is an everyday brand it would not be particularly exciting to stage an exhibition of product, and we didn't want to make a splash by staging an event using peripheral stuff like fleets of Minis or other British design icons.' So rather than try to jazz up collections of Habitat classics, Dixon felt it was an opportunity to try something new.

He explains why finding a common cause and direction in an international commercial outfit can be a challenge. 'The generic problem in a large organisation is that it tends to split into groups that have very different motivations and working practices the retail people have to be in the present, product development people have to look two years into the future and marketing people have to do something that is essentially less practical and concentrate on getting people excited about the brand rather than the day-to-day business of actually flogging stuff. So there are different outputs, structures and types of people with various priorities.' The triumph of the idea for the VIP range was that it appealed to everyone. 'Being realistic about it, not everybody is interested in 'design' itself, I wanted to talk to people who were not already converted, not just the interior décor crowd. Sports and celebrity are what most people are 'into' at home. We added an element of humour too, but at the same time made sure that everything was meticulously presented, from packaging to product photography, so that we could tell the story properly about all 20 objects.'

A good example of how a well-executed idea can capture the imagination of both those within a company and the general public; the VIP products flew off the shelves, and generated acres of press coverage, raising the profile of Habitat and helping to draw the distinction between it and other retailers operating in the same arena.

Looking more specifically at the task of working as Creative Director with the Habitat design team, Dixon's view is that the role is 'very much about knowing as much as possible and to see a pattern emerging from it, almost like chaos theory. You see a pattern, and try to refine it whilst keeping a healthy distance from the individual items… you don't want to get too stuck into one teapot, for example because you don't want to end up fighting the wrong battle…so it's very different to when I am working as a designer myself where you need to be obsessed with the object you're dealing with.'

He points out that the environment itself is not suited to all designers. 'It can be difficult for some to work within a retail organisation with an emphasis on commerce rather than a design

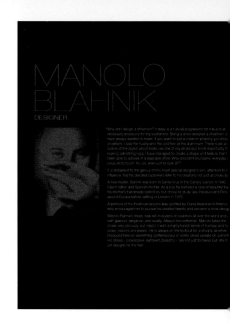

Above
Spread from the catalogue for Habitat's VIP range featuring the **Manolo Blahnik Shoehorn**

Right
Cone Light
Cone: Spun aluminium, black matt finish.
Diffuser: Opal Acrylic, gloss finish.
74cm diameter

Far right
Swarovski Chandelier

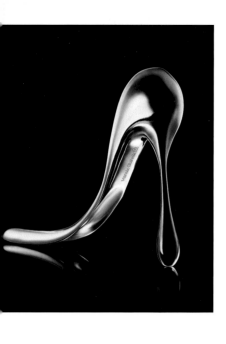

'… You see a pattern, and try to refine it whilst keeping a healthy distance from the individual items …'

– – – – – – – – – – – – – –

organisation, and which deals with literally thousands of objects each season. This can be a tough environment for designers to survive in; they can be in danger of becoming just processors of stuff.' He sees part of his role as creative director as 'preventing people from slipping onto the treadmill of borrowing or copying ideas, because that's not what Habitat is about; it must be original and creative.'

An added hurdle for the creative team is provided by an all-year round festive season, which would try the patience of most of us.' Sometimes it can be a little difficult to stay fresh because it is always Christmas. You are always doing one of three Christmas-related things; reviewing how things went last Christmas, launching for this one or planning for the next.'

In Dixon's own design work, a couple of examples show an inspired use of pure form; the glittering sphere chandelier for Swarovski and the Tom Dixon Cone Light are both statuesque in scale, but delicate in execution.

In many other projects his inspiration seems to lie in the way things are made, taking different production methods and using the process and materials involved to build new objects.' Dixon describes his hands-on methods with enthusiasm; 'Getting intimate with the manufacturing process and the possibilities of the material then defines the output in the long run...so that I get good at welding or blow-moulding or extruding and then I can design which makes my approach slightly different to other peoples.'

One material which Tom Dixon has explored shows both how one thing leads to another in his design work and highlights the importance of ongoing relationships with suppliers and manufacturers for a designer with such an emphasis on production. Dixon has experimented with plastic since relatively early success with the rotary-moulded Jack Light (which won him a 1997 Millennium Mark award).

More recently, he played with extrusion and set up a mini-factory in Selfridges's window and at the Milan furniture fair, squishing out loops of still-warm 'Fresh Fat Plastic' to be formed into customised shapes. (Gabriel Chemie, the Masterbatch producers who provide the dye for colour plastics sponsored the machine.) Dixon explained that 'this was a conversation about the nature of manufacturing. If you consider Habitat to be a shop, and Ikea a warehouse, then the next step for customers could be to deal direct with a factory. Many brands such as Levis and Smart cars are obsessed with customisation, and there's a good reason for that...it's not just that people want things to their own taste. If you could get to the point where you make things to order, people would pay in advance and no storage or stock levels are needed. We showed you could make furniture to order and deliver it hot off the press. We also illustrated that design can be hands-on. There is an artificial division between industry and craftsmanship and too many designers spend their whole lives at computers with no involvement in making.' It is indeed unusual to find a process associated with heavy industry such as extrusion used in a way that echoes basket weaving.

The use of extrusion and

'There is an artificial division between industry and craftsmanship and too many designers spend their whole lives at computers with no involvement in making.'

— — — — — — — — — — — — —

familiarity with its application led to the creation of the Extendable Screen, with modular construction inspired by a roll-up garage door. Provista PETG plastic was used which has 'a handmade quality — with stippling like stained glass'.

The collaboration with Gabriel Chemie as supplier 'and patron' developed further and Tom Dixon studio is working with the company at the moment on ingenious alternatives to the usual way in which colour and materials samples are given to potential customers. At the moment most suppliers provide small rectangular tablets with varying thicknesses, called 'tiles'. The idea is to make a structure built up of shaped pieces. 'From a practical point of view you might give your proper customers who place regular orders a huge geodesic dome with the full range of colours and finishes, whereas someone who needs a single colour would have a single tile.' The structure solves a practical issue, which is that plastic samples need to show colours as flat and curved surfaces. As you

Far left
Fresh Fat Easy Chair in construction

Left
Fresh Fat window in
Selfridge's store, London 2002

Below & bottom left
Extendable Screen
Provista/PETG copolyester
180 × 100 cm units
Assembled screen and
close-up of modular components

Bottom right
Work-in-progress for Gabriel Chemie

can see from the renderings of some initial ideas for the form the 'tiles' could build, the assembled result will give an eye-catching solution, which is a refreshing alternative to the industry norm of boring rectangular swatches. That is applied creativity at its best, clever and different.

In 2004 Tom Dixon's own design company joined forces with venerable Finnish furniture label Artek, to form a new company, 'Art & Technology'. The ingredients for success are all there: solid financial backing from Swedish private investment fund (Proventus) combined with the vision, determination and ambition of Dixon and his team. Expect to hear a lot more from Tom Dixon over the next few years.

* * *

www.habitat.net
www.artek.fi
www.tomdixon.net

39

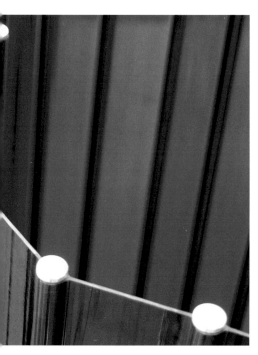

It's all Mushroom Girls and BoyLiness for designer Deanne Cheuk. With her obsessive illustration style, the art director for Tokion magazine and the self-published Neomu has been hailed a 'Graphic Wunderkind' in the Big Apple.

Deanne Cheuk

Interview by Lachlan Blackley

Originally from Australia you now live and work in New York. What's your Bright Lights Big City story? I'd always had aspirations of living in New York one day. When you come from a city like Perth you can dream such things but never imagine it would be possible. When I finally came here for a holiday in February 2000 I was so in love with everything about the city that I couldn't get it out of my mind and I moved here not long after. I think it's impossible not to be inspired in New York — you're surrounded by art, music and design, and people doing amazing things.

Where did you first work? Was it difficult to establish yourself? I was David Carson's assistant. He called me while I was still in Perth and I started to work with him pretty much straight away for about two years. I also started making illustrations when I first moved to NY, so that gradually picked up more and more work. And finally there came a day when I had too much work of my own to work for anyone else and that is where I am now.

Can you tell us the story behind Neomu? I call Neomu a 'graphic 'zine of inspiration'. It's a randomly published collection of pictures and illustrations that I compile from an open call for submissions. I started it in 2000 because I missed self-publishing and I still had all these great artists and designers I was in contact with when I published a magazine in Australia called 'Mu'.

Above left
Deanne Cheuk
Cover, Tokion Magazine No. 43
2004
Photographer: Stefan Ruiz

Above centre
Deanne Cheuk
Cover, Tokion Magazine No. 44
2004
Photographer: Kenneth Cappello

Above right
Deanne Cheuk
Neomu No. 01–07
Design & Illustrations by Deanne Cheuk

Right
Deanne Cheuk

THE SOUND OF NOW

'I have always been quite obsessed with inspiration. So with Neomu I really wanted to try to inspire every-one involved with it.'

— — — — — — — — — — — — —

OK, maybe we should begin with a little about Mu. I started Mu in 1997. It was a music, art and fashion magazine that I self-published for 5 issues. The last issue was published in 1999. I stopped it when it finally broke even and I decided to move on. It pretty much evolved from 'Mu' and that's why it's called 'Neomu'. I have always been quite obsessed with inspiration and trying to capture that. So with Neomu I really wanted to try to inspire everyone involved with it — from the artists that have their work published, to the stores that sell it for $1 and donate the proceeds to charities, to the charities that benefit from it. I never did it for myself and I think this is part of why it is has been so successful — because I've always approached it as a gift for others.

And the non-profit idea? That was part of the passing along of inspiration thing — it came about from not wanting to make Neomu a commercial venture. I pay for it entirely myself and send it to the stores for free, it's then up to them to donate proceeds to charities of

their choice.

Why the pocket book size? The size came about basically because I thought it would be cheaper! In the end it wasn't really. I made it the smallest size that my printer could notch bind at the time.

Is there a theme for each issue? There is never a theme, I just ask for submissions to be original and inspiring, I give a few words to think about each time like Light, Dark, Magic etc. But those are just starting points. By the time I put the submissions together I see some threads that are more prominent than others and that makes it easier to have the pages run together smoothly.

What do you most enjoy about producing Neomu? I just feel incredibly lucky to get to see all this amazing work each time I do an issue — there aren't enough pages to publish everything so there's a lot that no-one else gets to see but me. It's great when magazines and galleries contact me about getting in touch with artists from an issue. Neomu has become a bit of a source

book for contemporary illustrators. I think it's also a snapshot of what's happening at that particular time with illustration trends. I definitely see certain trends from issue to issue that evolve each time — it's really interesting. *Do you do all this yourself or does someone help you?* Myself! I work most hours of the day alone, the reality of it is very unglamorous!

You've art-directed and designed 13 or so magazines. What led you to work in the magazine industry and publish your own in the first place? It all just kind of happened. When I was still at University there was only one cool magazine coming out of Perth, called REVelation magazine. I interned there during my last year of study and by the time I graduated, they liked me so much they asked me to be the art director — I was 19 at the time. I did that for 3 years, and then went away on a 3 month holiday and while I was away it went out of business! So I came back and decided to start Mu. At that time it was a lot more unusual for someone to self-publish a magazine. Printing

AT THE CONTROLS

Who is it that makes a great album? The obvious answer is the artist in the studio and later performing the hits onstage. But in the background are the men at the controls, the producers and engineers who help shape and realize the performer's vision, and the records they have recorded rank as some of the best of all time: *A Love Supreme, My Generation, Exile On Mainstreet, Marquee Moon, Heroes, Fear of a Black Planet, Surfer Rosa* and many more. They may not be household names but their legacy will live on, etched in vinyl long after the spotlight fades.

'Inevitably you'll get the same idea at the same time as someone else. But that just drives me to keep trying, to get that new idea first.'

Photography by PETER STANGLMAYR
Stylist: Jay Massacret / Hair: Ramona @ Bumble & Bumble / Makeup: Yuko Washizu for Dior / Models: Brian @ Request, Gordon @ IMG
Spring/Summer 05 preview
GORDON WEARS SHORTS BY OPENING CEREMONY, NYLON JACKET

was less accessible, independent publishing was not as polished as what I was trying to produce. People were confused about where this magazine came from and what it was. I was doing everything myself, designing, editing, compiling, distribution. I was even trying to sell ads myself, can you imagine? It was a nightmare. Advertising executives had no interest in speaking to this young girl that kept calling them about this strange magazine. It was an uphill battle daily, but the end result was a great project that I owned and made and had complete control over. I will always think of it as the best thing I ever did.

What do you like most about art directing a magazine? At the moment I am really enjoying being able to do something different with magazine design and hopefully encourage others to approach their magazines the same way.

How have you seen your ideas and work develop as a result? The biggest development in my work has been in the past four years working as an illustrator. I think the looseness and expressiveness I've gained from illustrating is something I've been able to interpret in my graphic design and art direction for the better. A lot of my typography is about movement, like type that looks like it is smashed and coming off the page, or type that is organic and growing. This has all been a progression from my illustration work. I often see other people interpreting this in their own work, which is frustrating because I feel like they didn't go anywhere to come to that point.

Your work in Tokion is very fresh and creative. You often handcraft, draw and paint the titles for each feature. It must be very time-consuming. What led you to this approach? It is incredibly time consuming. Some title pages can take me days to do or days to be happy with. I only get a week to design the magazine so it can be quite an intense week. For some warped reason, a part of me still believes that if I do it in a simple or basic way, then it's too easy or it's cheating. I know that's ridiculous but I'll print out the page and look at it and think, no, that's boring, and then spend all night doing something insanely intricate and over the top! I've created a monster!

It seems people are embracing this warmer handcrafted approach to design. WWD [Womenswear Daily] magazine last week acknowledged that the trend of hand drawing in layouts started 'downtown' in New York with Tokion Magazine, so that's cool! It's all been a natural progression from my illustration work. I don't buy other magazines or design books, so I don't feel like I am really influenced by other design trends. There is always the collective consciousness where inevitably you'll get the same idea at the same time as someone else. But that just drives me to keep trying, to be thinking further ahead, to get that new idea first before it's already out there.

Do you feel a pressure to be ahead of the game? Honestly, no. It's really nice for people to recognise my work, but at the same time I know the reality is very unglamorous!

So what stimulates you visually/creatively? Old books. I can spend hours in second hand bookstores. That's all really. I look at everything else — other media — but when I need to sit down and start something new, I'll always go back to my bookshelves. I just got a great book today called 'How to tell fortunes by reading tea leaves' — the patterns of the leaves in the book are so nice, I already got so many ideas just from looking at it really quickly.

Your style and subject is very organic. Where else do you get your ideas? Nature, the movement of the ocean, waves, surf, birds — flight patterns, wing shapes, colours…I get a lot of my colours from birds.

Are there artists or designers that have had an influence on what you do? Not to a profound extent, but definitely some inspiration has come from Tadanori Yokoo and Aquirax Uno. Tadanori Yokoo blows me away with his whole body of work. When I first came across his work in Japan it was the first time I ever thought of working with collage, as he is the king! Aquirax Uno's work is harder to come by. His drawings are amazing; they're really psychedelic and look very contemporary though he is from the 60s. I think a lot of illustrators are inspired by his style but he doesn't seem to be credited for it.

'Mushroom Girls Virus' is your latest exhibition and book release. This is quite a beautiful

Far left
Deanne Cheuk
Page 36, Tokion Magazine No. 43
2004

Left
Deanne Cheuk
Page 25, Tokion Magazine No. 43
2004

Below
Deanne Cheuk
Pages 104–105, Tokion Magazine No. 44
2004
Photographer: Peter Stranglmayr

Issue Seven—Graphic Magazine
Show+Tell+Profile

Left & above
Deanne Cheuk
Mushroom Girls Virus Book
Illustrations
2004

Issue Seven—Graphic Magazine
Show+Tell+Profile

Liness

OwLiness Fall 2004 www.liness.net

Opposite page, top
Liness BoyLiness Spring 05 Collection
2004
Client: Liness
Design by Deanne Cheuk, Rilla Alexander
& Yasmin Majidi
Photos by Pierrre Toussaint

Opposite page, bottom, & this page
Liness OwLiness Fall 04 Collection
2004
Client: Liness
Design by Deanne Cheuk, Rilla Alexander
& Yasmin Majidi
Photos by Pierrre Toussaint

'It's a bit of a chain reaction I've been on for many years now. I'm waiting for it to stop sparking but it seems to keep going.'

and sensual series of images. What's it all about? I was first making illustrations of girls and mushrooms about 2 years ago. I was already drawing girls and I really liked the colours and textures of mushrooms and I guess the style developed quite quickly into what I started to call my 'Mushroom Girls'. I was invited to have a solo show at the 222 Gallery in Philadelphia in August 2004 and the book was a compilation of my work in the year leading up to preparing for the show. It's a lot of drawings, paintings and collages and ideas around the theme of 'Mushroom Girls'.

Where did the ideas originate? From a colour, from a paint drip, from a line, a piece of cloth, from anything.

Why a book? Well, for me it felt like my diary for the year, this is the work I spent so many hours on. I wanted to compile everything into one book to capture that phase of my work. The cover is pink cloth and it is fully embroidered — I am really happy with the cover most of all, it feels precious and almost secretive.

Can you explain further your involvement and experience with fashion as a graphic designer and illustrator? I've always loved fashion and it's an area I have wanted to work in for a while. It's almost like the ultimate compliment when someone likes your graphic so much that they will pay for it and walk around in it!

You're known also for your T-shirt designs. What's cool about the whole T-shirt thing for you? I do T-shirts for Tsubi, 2K and Stüssy and in the past have done them for Abahouse, Levis Strauss Japan and Oki-Ni. I like doing them because they can be quite random and in a style that I wouldn't normally work in. Especially when it's men's T-shirts — my work is never masculine, so it's refreshing to switch sometimes.

What's your favourite T-shirt? Anything by Liness of course! My current favourite is a reworking we did of a Joy Division graphic, which says 'Boy Division'.

'Liness' is a collection you've started with Rilla Alexander and Yasmin Majidi. Can you tell us more? I've known Rilla [Rinzen] for a while and we were always talking about our experiences with clothing companies. And it was just a natural progression for us to both go out on our own and start a label where we would have complete control over the look and quality and product. I knew Yasmin for a while too and always admired her as a fashion designer, so we all decided to work together on a line.

What's the idea behind the name? This season is 'OwLiness'. The name of the brand 'Liness' is a made up word. It works as a suffix to each season's theme, like OwLiness and BoyLiness. BoyLiness is our Spring 2005 collection, which is all about being obsessed with boys. Each range is a different obsession.

What direction do you hope this takes? At the moment we're making really wearable but memorable and creative pieces that we would want to wear ourselves, it seems to be working so far, so we'll keep at it!

You must be constantly working. What drives you? I am constantly working, yes it's a bit sad, but true! I think I am really driven by my own work. You know, you make something that looks really cool and you think, 'wow, now what if I try this?' And that sparks something else. It's a bit of a chain reaction I've been on for many years now. I'm waiting for it to stop sparking but it seems to keep going, luckily for me!

Is design all-consuming for you? What do you do in your time off? I took two weeks off last month, went back to Perth and just did nothing but draw pictures all day long, which of course I brought back to NY and scanned in and used for many different jobs. So I guess I don't really take time off. The thing is that I don't really get too wound

48

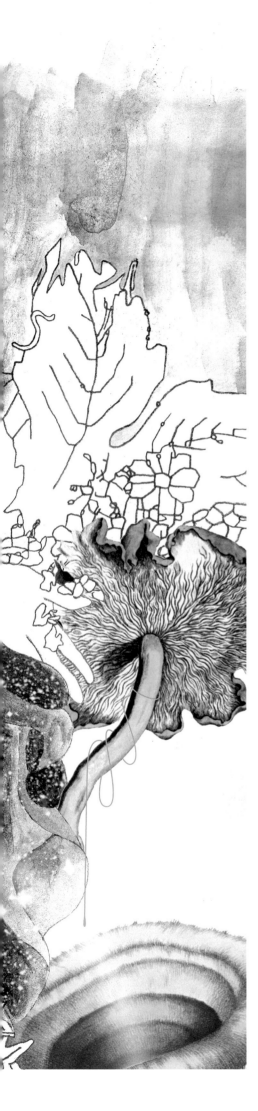

> 'I did Mu at a time that independent publishing in Australia was virtually non-existent. Even though I was told not to, I still did it.'

— — — — — — — — — — — — —

up as such, so I don't need to wind down. I find it quite relaxing to be working, it's very enjoyable and I do such a variety of work that it keeps me constantly interested. I was travelling every two months for the last two years doing art direction for Urban Outfitters and the last trip we did was to Iceland — so even when it's work, it doesn't always feel like it!

Can you talk a little about your work for Urban Outfitters? I was art directing their catalogues. It was 6 catalogues a year, 60 pages, 12 million copies; it was one of my biggest jobs for a while. I just stopped recently to spend more time on Liness. It was really fun working with Urban Outfitters but it was just too much work for one person. On top of that was all my other work and Tokion — working with 2 print deadlines simultaneously. I don't know how I did it!

What do you enjoy most about having your hand in so many areas? The variety, it keeps me sane and it keeps the jobs feeling fresh. By the time another Tokion deadline comes around I will have designed another clothing collection, travelled to a photo shoot in another city, designed this that and the other, and be ready and more inspired than ever to start on a new issue.

Looking at your career so far, what are you most proud of? I'll always be the proudest of Mu magazine. That was something I started and put everything into and kept working on even when I felt like no one cared or understood it. I did it at a time that independent publishing in Australia was virtually non-existent, and even though I was told not to do it — I still did it!

Plans for 2005? Just more of the same!

Finally, what's Deanne Cheuk's utopic vision? Flowers, gigantic, everywhere…and girls and mushrooms of course!

* * *

www.neomu.com
www.mushroomgirlsvirus.com
www.liness.net

Left
Deanne Cheuk
Mushroom Girls Illustration
2003–2004
Client: Nylon Magazine

After my pleasant stay in Ivö, I came to the conclusion that the world is divided into two kinds of people
living on opposite sides and I immediately found myself enjoying the stay on the weaker side.
The first kind is like the honey bee. He lives his life looking for the sweeter aspects,
making sweet things such as honey – respecting others, working hard, enjoying life
in the community, saving his money and protecting his leader.
This kind of people, who live like honey bees, are not as dangerous as might be expected.
Alright, they might be gloriously noisy but that's about the only trouble they can cause.
The second type is like the bear, I mean, wild and greedy bears, attracted to golden honey.
They are powerful and smart and have developed their sense of smell to lead them straight to life's
treasures while destroying entire communities and their savings. Money bears can't fly
because their conscience is too heavy. They can only walk flat on land, more often than not,
on all fours. They are brown but if you meet them at twilight, just after seven o'clock,
you may notice how their colour turns into a shining gold, and well,
just make sure they've already got their dinner on the table.

Typography 01 (this spread): I want your money / I want your honey
Typography 02 (spread forward): I am a money bear / I am a honey bee

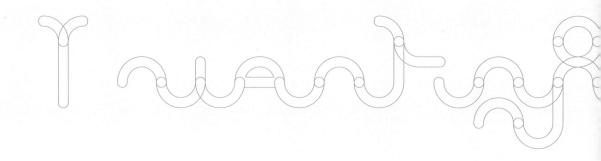

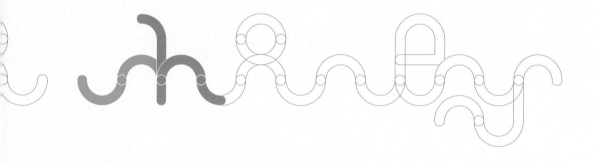

07:00 pm

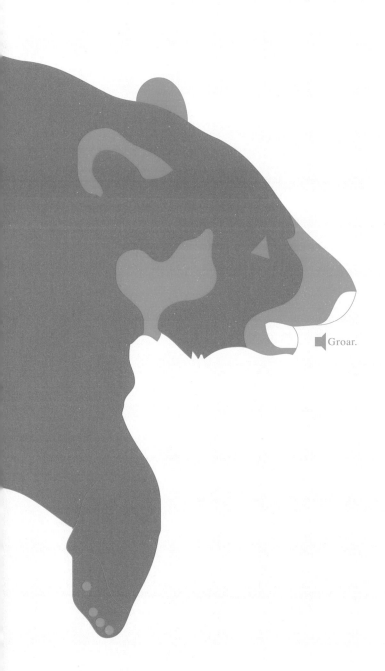

Groar.

I am a sh

Honey, Bears and Mr Jan Falck
11.2004

That evening, in Ivö, it was a little bit cold but the air was dry. I was having a pleasant dinner outside in the garden with my hosts, a Swedish family, who were putting me up for the night on my way to Norrland. While driving up from Italy to the northern part of Sweden, I had intended to take some pictures with my new Holga camera to make into a sort of story which I could send in to magazines. However, two things didn't quite work out as planned. First, handling a Holga for the first time can lead to all sorts of surprises when it comes to film processing and second, I got extremely involved in a very long conversation about bees with Mr Jan Falck. He told me practically everything he knew about honey, community life, protection and queens. Somewhere along the way, the new Holga began to lose its attraction and golden bears began floating around in my mind.

When asked to name his price,
Giuliano Garonzi replied: Two weeks in Mexico with my sweetheart, Stella!

Giuliano was born in 1974 and raised in Veron He lived in a 90m² apartment with his father and shared a bedroom with his older brother. The grey and pink building was located on a street named after the talented Italian typographer, Bodoni. On the left side of the road were the apartment blocks and on the right the printing works of Italy's largest publishers. Giuliano remembers how on summer nights the air was filled with the noise of the offset printers, running at a speed of 15,000 copies an hour. Giuliano knew all along that having grown up on that street, so close to the printers, educated by a graphic designer father and having a brother who worked in graphic arts as a room mate, he stood absolutely no chance of becoming a cook instead of a graphic designer. Today, Giuliano is now part of the multi-disciplinary design studio Happycentro+Sintetik in Verona, working on fashio projects and collaborating with agencies such as McCann Erickson and Publicis.

giulianogaronzi@happycentro.it
www.happycentro.it

01

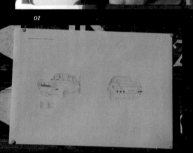

03

05

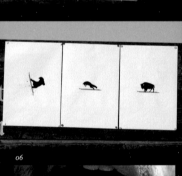

06

04

08

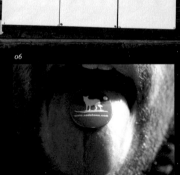

07

00

My.K
Born in 1978
From Tokyo, Japan

Achievements
2002 POL Oxygen
2000 etisoppo vol.1&2

asaginuya@hotmail.com
www.page.sannet.ne.jp/my-k/

When asked to name her price,
Mai Kuwahata replied: My price isn't given. My
value is 1,000,000 euro by the person, and it is
wasteful to pay 1 euro, too, but it is worthwhile.

Money fate
25.11.2004

The image that I drew is the one said to improve
money fates [luck with money] in Japan. People
put their wishes in the cat, the ship, and the
cleaning tools in Japan so that their money fate
may improve.

00

01

02

03

04

05

06

07

08

00
My.K

01
The guitar is in a bad mood

02
Glasses

03
Kimono and machine gun

04
Little Red Riding Hood

05
Tanabata

06
Soda pop

07
In the sky

08
Festival

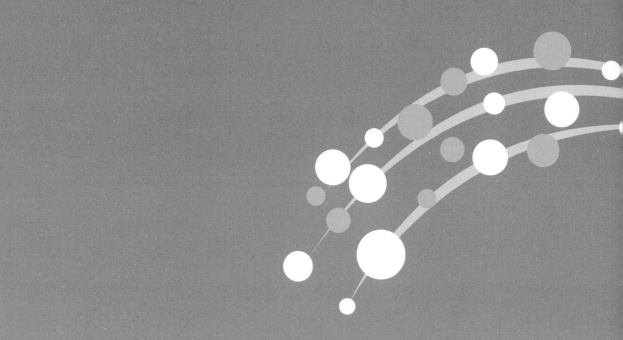

Stay at Homes
2004

I started making these studies of cutout floral ornamentation to use in my larger works. These were made on pieces of scrap paper from around the studio. Cleaning the studio I found an old Penthouse magazine from 1977 that I had. There is an adolescent nostalgia in those pages, I mean, healthy or not, these were what formulated my early ideas of sexuality. I later took some pages out and, putting them under the smaller drawn studies, did this cut paper thing I do. When I painted them I laughed to think I was the second-generation of airbrush to have laid paint to these images.

A year later I am still at it, creating these smaller works alongside my larger pieces for exhibitions. Something is interesting here, back and front…

When asked to name his price,
Reed Anderson replied: a bowl of hot soup

I was born in New York City in 1969. I spent a lot of time making drawings and forts around my house, which is pretty much what I do now. There was a variety of modern art on our walls and it was fun to arrange it in different ways adding my own work. It was a good childhood.

In my work I am seeking to combine school-desk-notebook graffiti and early American craft to create some new visual beast. To illustrate that the cheap and the sacred share the same bed. Currently I am interested in simple line drawings and their transformation through the arabesque (lines become ornamented flora and fauna). The drawings are cut and stenciled onto themselves. This self-generating mutation allows for a transcendental experience, whereby the initial image is secondary to the experience of the whole. Where Psychedelic-Rorschach meets Animal-Baroque for a steel cage match.

iamreed@earthlink.net
www.reedanderson.info
www.Pierogi2000.com
www.feigencontemporary.com

01

00

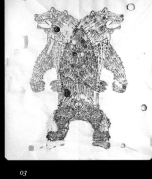

02

04

03

06

07

05

08

00
Reed Anderson
Photo: Todd Crawford

01
Cruel Hoax
2002
Collage, acrylic paint & airbrush on cut paper
76" × 66.5"

02
Et Nunc Et Semper (for J.L.S.)
2004
Collage, acrylic paint & airbrush on cut paper
26" × 28"

03
Chinese Hemisphere
2003
Collage, acrylic paint & airbrush on cut paper
96" × 84"

04
Funny-Cry-Happy
2003
Collage, acrylic paint & airbrush on cut paper
55" × 57.5"

05
Thank You Lover
2004
Collage, acrylic paint & airbrush on cut paper
56" × 59"

06
Siesta 69
2003
Collage, acrylic paint & airbrush on cut paper
59" × 55"

07
Tippy Trip
2003
Collage, acrylic paint & airbrush on cut paper
96" × 84"

08
Locker Tsunami
2002
Collage, acrylic paint & airbrush on cut paper
66" diameter

0.0441 DIOR HANDBAGS
IN NEW YORK

Nawel

Nawel was born in 1973, in Neuilly sur Seine, France. She has been interested in anything that's art, from a very young age on. Frequent visits to the museum revealed her vocation of everything that had something to do with 'image'. She studied at the 'Beaux Arts' in Paris, design, architecture, history of art, fashion …

All these different aspects give her a flexibility and curiosity, which allows her to work in many ways and forms. Diversity and renewal are the principal motivations in her work. Her research in body language and image, conducted her towards fashion. She first became a designer for men's collections for Guy Laroche, then a stylist for photographers, casting and production for Hermès, PR for Fifi Chachnil …

Her work is now based on the image of fashion, with which Nawel develops a symbiosis between her classical background and renewing it with a fashionable style. She created a very personal style working with many different techniques, painting, photography, photomontage, drawing …

Her true aspirations are emotion, timelessness and the desire to transcend the reflection beyond appearances.

When asked to name her price, Nawel replied: I hate speaking about money, ask my agent!

Photo/paint: Nawel
Styling: Kanako B. Koga @ Studio G
Photo assistant: Grigori Rassinier
Make up: Tatsu Yamanaka @ Marie-France
Hair: Tomohiro @ Olga
Styling assistant: Sohei Yoshida
Production: Sophie Glanddier & Amaury van Ryswyck @ Spine
Retouch: Pierrick @ keepcoul
Studio: Digitline Studio

00

01

02

03

04

05

06

07

00
Nawel

01
Chaussures Dior
Paint & artwork by Nawel
Photo: Cecile Bortoletti
Stylist & model: Masha Orlov
Red leather sandals with flowers, Christian Dior Haute Couture by John Galliano

02
Coiffe Lacroix
Paint & artwork by Nawel
Photo: Cecile Bortoletti
Stylist & model: Masha Orlov
Hat with fringes, ribbons and fur: Christian Lacroix
Haute Couture

03
Bodies
Photos & artwork by Nawel
Stylist: Hortense Manga
Pearled satin red dress, Veronique Branquinho; golden silk top and taffeta skirt, Louis Vuitton; vintage cap, Guy Laroche; wool jumper with rhinestones, Sonia Rykiel; bikini bottom with rhinestones, Sonia Rykiel; black veil, Lanvin; pearl necklace, Chanel; silk jacket, Givenchy; bikini, Omok

04
Portrait Lacroix
Paint & artwork by Nawel
Photo: Cecile Bortoletti
Stylist & model: Masha Orlov
Pink silk quilted and laméd coat worn with pink silk and lace slipdress, Christian Lacroix Haute Couture; black crystal earring, Christian Lacroix Haute Couture

05
Redress
Photos & artwork by Nawel
Stylist: Hortense Manga
Red muslin dress with green elastic belt, Versus; georgette lurex jacket and lurex miniskirt, Rochas

06
Simple 01
Photos & artwork by Nawel
Stylist: Emma Tissandier
Chemise imprimée en popeline de coton, Prada; *jupe plissée en toile de coton*, Prada Sport; bracelets, Bala Boosté

07
Simple 04
Photos & artwork by Nawel
Stylist: Emma Tissandier
Top en lin et coton, Hussein Chalayan; *pull col V en coton*, Gianfranco Ferré; *Short imprimé en coton*, Bless; *foulard en soie*, Hermès; mocassins, Miu Miu; *sac multipoches*, Prada

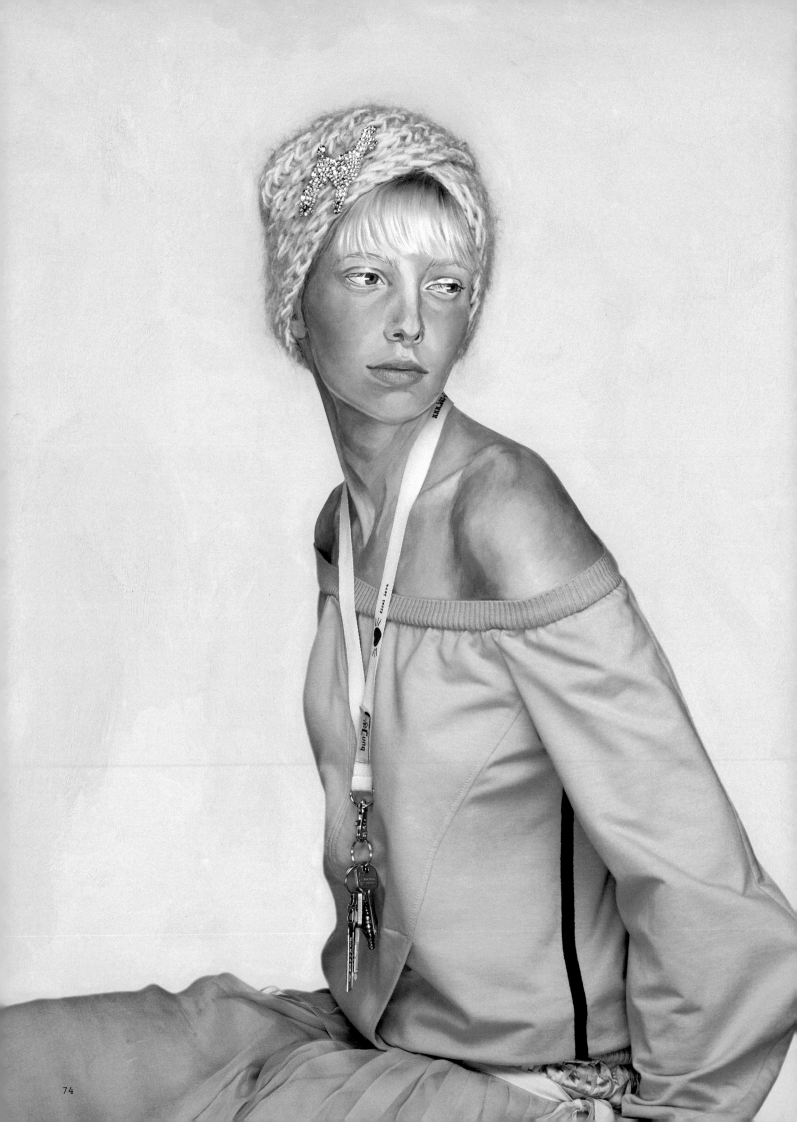

Ernst Fischer

Still Life With Toaster
11.2004
A vanitas still life in the ambiguous spirit of the
Flemish masters, alluding to the polarity of life
and death by the use of symbols of either personal
or universal validity: fruit, sweetest just before it
rots, futile accumulation of riches, guarded by
locusts, a melancholy hare with a soft, cold snout,
various civilisatory implements, passed down the
family tree, and the man in the cabbage, who has
followed me 'round for as long as I can remember, forever locked in his silent holler.

When asked to name his price,
Ernst Fischer replied: … hell, no.

Ernst Fischer was born in Switzerland. He lives
and works in London.

www.ernstfischer.com

00

01

02

03

04

05

06

00
Ernst Fischer

01
From 'The Four Temperaments': Markus, choleric

02
From 'Land of Milk', an ongoing book project
about Switzerland

03
From the Trees of London series, nightly portraits
of trees that were dragged from the colonies and
have patiently suffered and survived generations of
English gardeners

04
From 'The English Landscape', a series reflecting on
life after Constable

05–06
From a visual diary about Uzbekistan: the last place
you'd want to look

Gum

Since GUM's initial release in 2002, this unique annual – covering art, design, pop culture, social issues and more – has attracted a very loyal fan base. In a market flooded with gorgeous design books short on substance at one end and content-driven publications lacking humour and aesthetic savvy at the other, GUM bridges the gap between style and content. The most recent issue features Ray Bradbury, Nancy Sinatra, Dalek, Nonconceptual, Rudy VanderLans, Interpol, Cornelius and more. Recently GUM launched its own creative agency, HIRED GUM.

editors@gumweb.com
www.gumweb.com

When asked to name their price,
Colin Metcalf and Kevin Grady replied:
Buy one, get one free

The Art of Bav-Go
2004
Is Bav-Go for real, or is he merely a figment of GUM's overactive imaginations, as some critic have claimed? Either way, there is simply no greater artist, living or dead, working in pancak

00

01

03

04

05

02

06

07

08

09

00
GUM founders Colin Metcalf and Kevin Grady

01
GUM1
the debut issue

02
Contents of GUM2

03
Counter display boxes for GUM1

04
GUM2

05
PLAYGUM
Limited-edition action figures.
Modelled by Sculpt This

06–07
GUM Mascots
'Big eye' versions of the Bionic Bigfoot Twins and their robotic sidekicks, Singolo and Dopio.
Illustrations by Greg Ruhl

08
Fred Was Here by Kevin Grady
Each custom-knit cardigan represents a decade of Mister Roger's Neighborhood.
Photograph by Dave Bradley

09
Neighbor by Colin Metcalf
A seven-foot diameter transportable memorial garden honoring the late host of Mister Roger's Neighborhood.
Photograph by Steven Barston

The Art of Bav-Go

"The first great artist of the 21st Century. Bav-Go fuses the technical mastery of a medium not seen since Gerhard Richter, with a raw, expressive immediacy rivaling Jean-Michel Basquiat in his pre-death period. There is simply no greater artist, living or dead, working in pancake." –<u>Art Semiotics Quarterly</u>

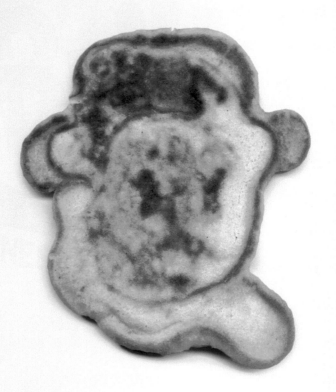

WINSTON S. CHURCHILL, IMMORTAL PROTECTOR OF THE REALM: A YOUTH INTERRUPTED / 2002
Batter and safflower oil on Calphalon, courtesy of the GUM Collection

A meditation on Britain's saviour of the Twentieth Century and the adolescence he relinquished to assume that destiny. The artist insists the ghostly apparition of Li'l Abner within the image was coincidence. Insiders believe it a clue to Bav-Go's own identification with a youth sacrificed in pursuit of greatness.

22

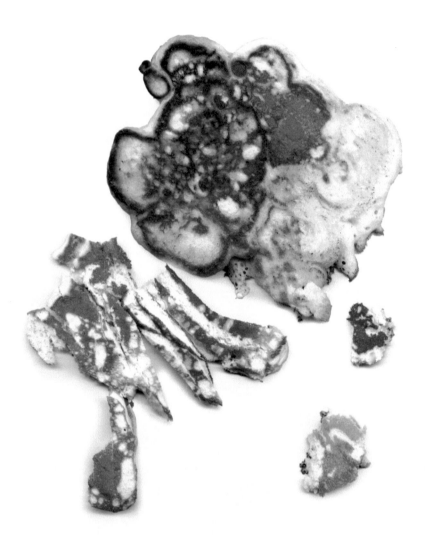

WOMAN I / 2003
Batter and whipped butter on Teflon, courtesy of the GUM Collection

A glimpse into the emotional chaos and savage torment defining his brief relationship with Nigella Lawson, this work lays bare a roiling confusion and frustration with the opposite sex. Evincing once again a prodigy which defies category, Bav-Go here transforms himself into a master of raw, abstract, edible emotion, thwarting critics who defined him too narrowly as a literalist.

23

THE ART OF BAV-GO

THE SHAPE OF FEAR: TRINITY, NEW MEXICO, 1945 / 1995
Batter and safflower oil on Teflon. From the Shape of Fear Series,
courtesy of the GUM Collection

Bav-Go's obsession with raw, explosive power is explored here in this, the artist's first work
following his dismissal from the U.S. Postal Service early in his career.

MAX BID: $45,000

THE SHAPE OF FEAR: BROCCOLI, DINNER, 1972 / 1995
Batter and safflower oil on Calphalon. From the Shape of Fear Series, courtesy of the GUM Collection

Bav-Go delves yet deeper into the dark themes of domination and subjugation, immortalizing an indelible image from childhood.

25

Pelé

$ MAX:
$65,000

PELÉ –THE BOY FROM BRAZIL! / 1999
Batter and I Can't Believe It's Not Butter on cast-iron griddle,
courtesy of the GUM Collection

A pure celebration of sport. Bav-Go became a Brazil fan when his German grandfather sent him
newspaper clippings from hiding as a child.

26

WOMAN II, RECONCILIATION / 2004
Bisquik batter, margarine and pork on Teflon, courtesy of the GUM Collection

While still clearly wrestling with his emotions towards the women in his life, this work finds the artist's relationships in a place of détente, if not absolute harmony. A certain optimism can be inferred by his cheekiness here. This work is widely regarded as the beginning of his confident Pig 'n' Blanket Period, entering its third week.

27

Value and Service

Burn, cut, release, dribble, spray, smash
Photography: Leon Chew

When asked to name their price,
Sean Murphy and Hazel Rattigan replied:
£60 per hour

Value and Service is a graphic design practice. Established in 2002 by Sean Murphy and Hazel Rattigan, V&S have since been designing/art directing for a broad variety of clients and requirements. The two met at college (CSM/RCA), working intermittently on projects over this period, after which their paths parted (Murphy worked at North design, Rattigan at David James Associates), before reconvening in 2002 to set up V&S.

info@valueandservice.co.uk
www.valueandservice.co.uk

01

02

03

04

05

06

07

08

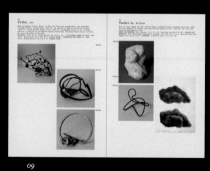

09

00
Sean Murphy and Hazel Rattigan

01
Bootleg invitation
Invitation to one-day art event in Spitalfields, London. Laserprinted onto high-end fashion ads cut from Vogue.

02–03
Contemporary Art Society report
Embossed vinyl cover and spread

04
Sure Thing poster
Poster for a theatre company. Overprinting fluorescent rainbow paper (created specifically for Sure Thing Productions) with images which describe the titles of the plays.
Design & photography: V&S

05
HP inspire poster
Poster to promote new design competition. Graphic language is based upon the award designed for the winner.
Art direction: V&S
Photography: John Short

06
Selfridges window
A window display on London's Oxford Street using materials normally found in window displays (vinyl, suckers, tape, whitewash etc.) to reproduce other shops' window displays. Each element was built up using layers of coloured vinyl, with a final layer of black or white stuck over the top creating a ghostly relief image.

07
Next Level flyposters
Posters to promote issue #6 of photography magazine Next Level, also designed by V&S.

08–09
Tom Bendhem exhibition catalogue
Catalogue for a travelling show of Tom Bendhem's collection of contemporary art, which was bequeathed to the Contemporary Art Society. The catalogue is printed mono onto buff stock, with colour plates glued over some layouts, referencing the art enthusiast's catalogues of the turn of the last century.

Issue Seven—Graphic Magazine
Look+Read+Use

0.0003 PORSCHE 911 CARRERAS
IN LONDON

Matthias Hoene

following pages [98-103]

A man of many talents, Matthias is not only known to direct music videos and commercials but has recently been a high-achieving participant in the 2004 South Yorkshire Gurning Competition.

Clearly, this man aims straight for the top but nevertheless his big ambitions are backed up by a big heart: he also runs a deaf people's telephone helpline and is a benefactor of the McDonald's Heart Disease Foundation.

How can a man of so many social engagements find time to do any honest work?

We asked that question as well and suspect that underpaid Chinese worker drones have actually produced all the pieces of work on this page. I hope you enjoy it anyway and you are welcome to send letters of complaint to his email address.

mail@matthiashoene.com
www.matthiashoene.com

When asked to name his price, Matthias Hoene replied: I escort high-achieving businesswomen who are in need of any kind of luxury evening entertainment. My clients tend to lead a balanced life and have reached a level of success that allows them to enjoy nothing but the finest pleasures in life. Being a discreet gentleman, I only negotiate prices with my clients directly. I charge by the hour, per day or for weekly call-outs.

When Bling Goes Blong
2004

Throughout East London the phenomena of 'blong blong' is spreading: it's the lifestyle of the 'nouveaux non riche' – people with high ambitions but with no taste and not that much money to back them up either. Go down to Ridley Road market, get yourself some gold rings, and join the fun. Pick up the car to suit your lifestyle from T-Flex at Fit & Last Garage just off Mare Street.

Photos by Matthias Hoene
Featuring: Billy Taylor @ Ugly and Michelle Killick @ Rage

Styling by Annabel Bonnett
Assistant: Hannah Stanton

Car sponsored by Fit & Last Garage,
24–26 Lamb Lane, Hackney E8 3PL

00

01

02

03

04

05

06

07

08

00
Matthias Hoene

01–08
A few stills from videos and commercials for Kristian Leontiou (01–03), The Mizchif Makaz (04–05) and Playstation (06–08).

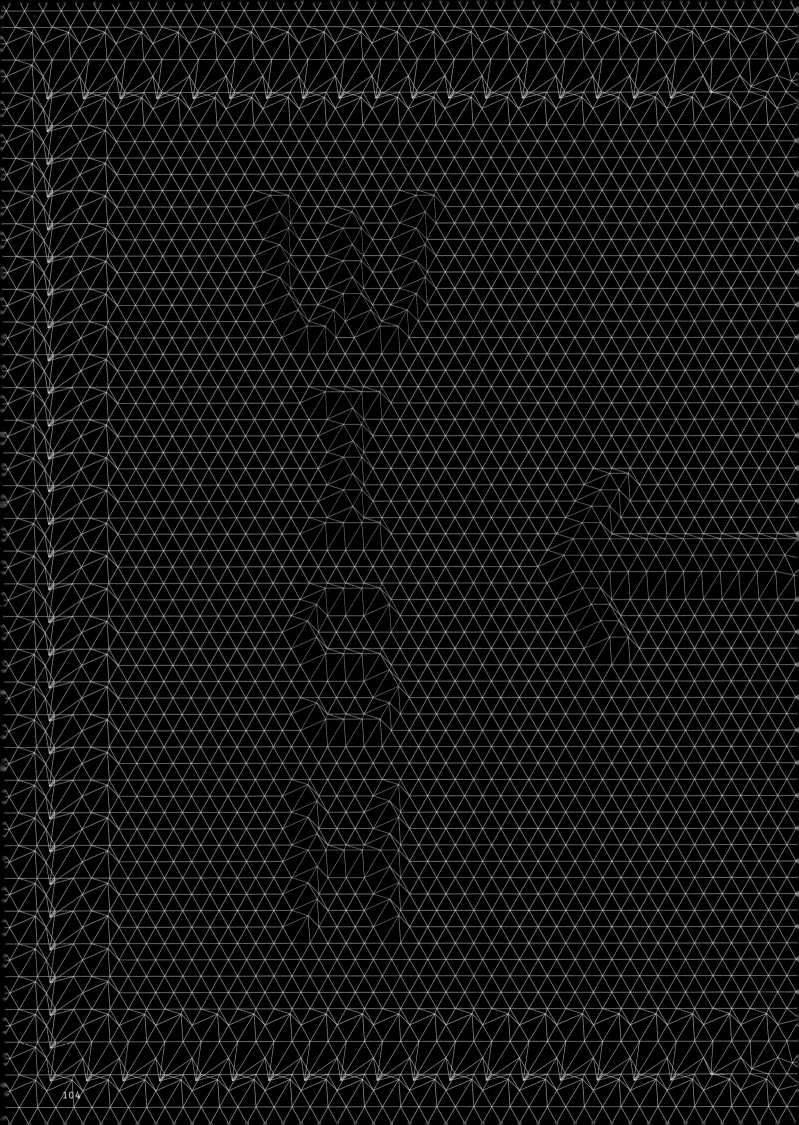

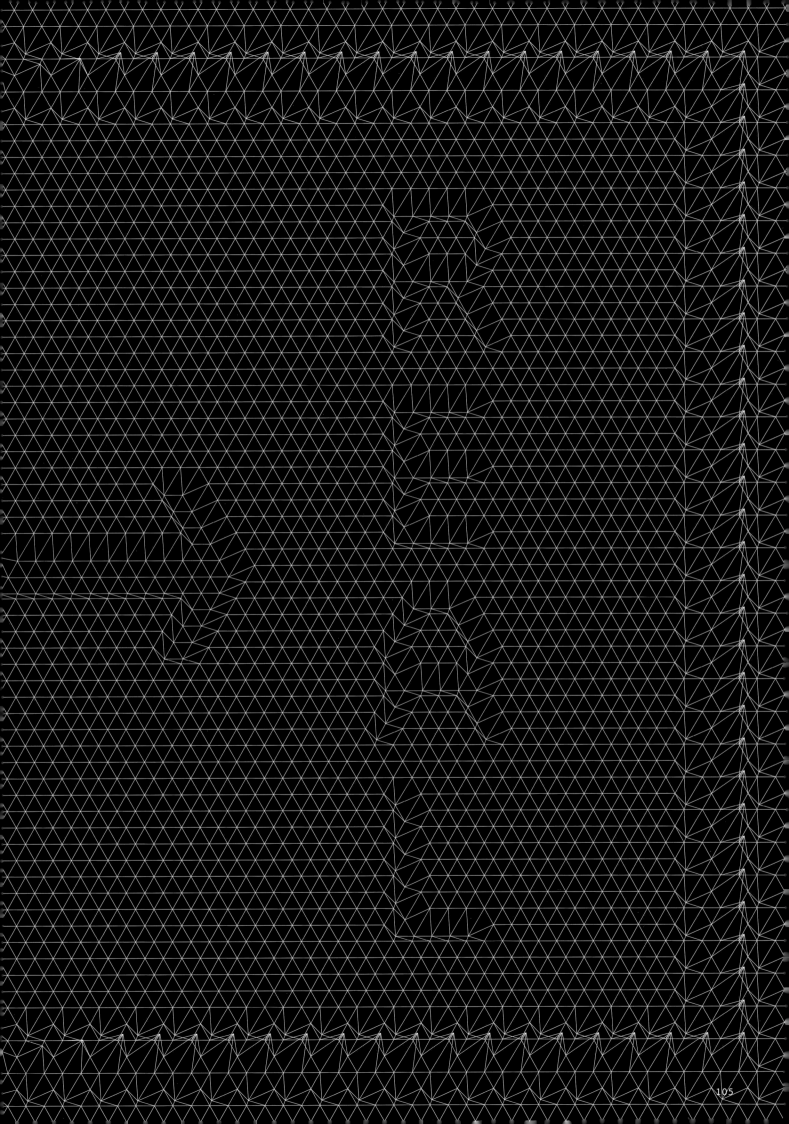

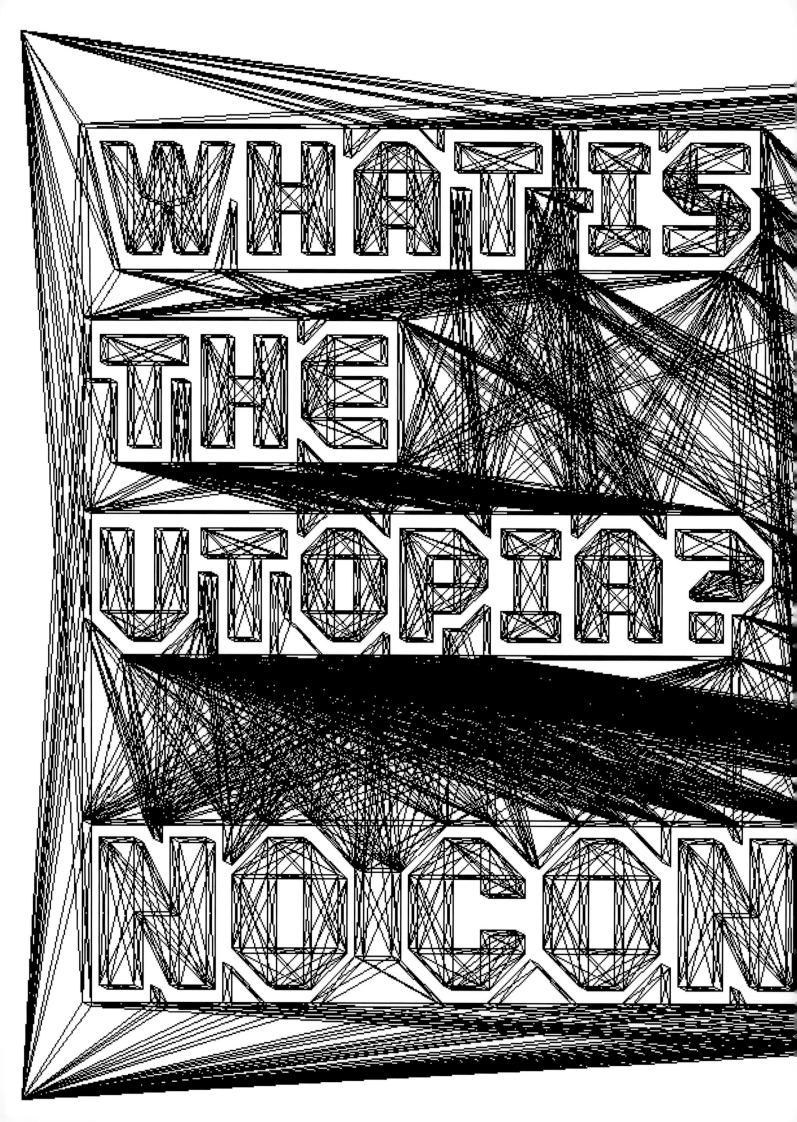

Human beings always want to know what it is worth. However, we always find difficulty everyday between 'wish' + 'reality', 'dream' + 'money'. And now, so many people are in the terrible war, they even don't have the time to think about the meaning of their life. So much confusion in the world. So many battles against identities.

There is a problem of identity in Japan. After the second World War, Japanese lifestyle changed a lot. When I was born, Japanese traditional life had already gone, it had been changed on to lifestyle which was Americanised. So, I haven't thought about what my Japanese background is. If we ask relatively younger Japanese 'what is your Japanese identity?', this question would perplex almost all of them. If I talk about graphics in Japan, now we are able to see any graphics and art in the world, thanks to the development of media, art and graphic design from overseas having a great influence on many Japanese graphic designer. (I went to London, because British graphic design had an effect on my graphics). Some younger designers are conscious of what 'Japanese' means to them, but the majority of them are not. However, Japanese graphics are different from those of other countries. So I think our activities of making graphics are the same as looking for the new Japanese identity.

When asked to name their price,
Megumu Kasuga, Mari Kobayashi and Minoru Dodo replied:
What's your system of values?
Satisfaction.
Is money everything?
No.
And if not, then what's your currency?
There is the leeway and the leisure to enjoy my life. There is the time to think about my family, my friends and my colleagues, then if I can enjoy working, it could be great.
What's your utopia?
No confusion. Everyone is laughing.
What's your dream?
Someone likes my works.
What's it worth?
Identity.

In 2001, three students at the Royal College of Art (London) got together.

Megumu Kasuga from the Communication Art & Design department, and another two from the Product Design department and the Computer Related Design department. After moving its base from London to Tokyo, Kasuga is now undertaking various activities with two new members – Minoru Dodo and Mari Kobayashi. (The other two original members have left the group and are doing inspiring activities in their own field now.)

We all have different backgrounds, so we've got various points of view from a variety of directions, and then, we want audiences to feel something of sensitive matters as we do by visual communication.

We mainly have our own projects for our clients in Europe. And we've recently worked for Japanese clients. Also, IdN Special 05 (book design & art direction) T-shirt design, and Logo design for a brand called '100%', Tokyo Typo Directors Club 2003 and 2004 Awards, etc.

yield_cad@yahoo.co.jp

01

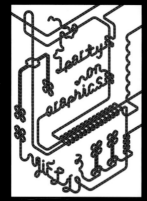
03

02

05

00

06

04

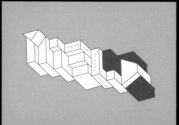

Federico Galvani

following pages [112-117]

I live and work in the lovely town of Romeo & Juliet. Since 1998, I share the experience of Happycentro+Sintetik project with a bunch of friends. One month ago we bought a bagatelle and this piece started to be a quality maker of our daily coffee breaks.

I love (more and more) my sweetheart Chiara, I have a brother, a sister, 3 nephews, many friends, an old blue car with a broken cd player in it, the same red Pumas since 10 years, a website, a passion for cheese and wax records, a green cantina in which I used to play my music, a bad English, a baby face, a father somewhere still looking after me. And all of this got no price for me.

federicogalvani@happycentro.it
www.happycentro.it

When asked to name his price,
Federico Galvani replied: a new shining pair of red Pumas.

No price
11.2004

To be overwhelmed by passion coming from a strong love story, having a family behind me and friends all around, have no price. No money can pay back a betrayed feeling between people. These spreads pretend to show that the best part of my life is deeper than everything else and most of the times I can reach that just behind a golden surface.

00

03

01

02

04

05

06

07

08

09

00
Federico Galvani

01
Wella/Welonda/BLOCKS
Brand image and various communication projects

02
Regione Veneto
'No doping' social ad campaign

03
Villa Cian
Fall winter flyer for an Italian club

04
Regione Veneto
'Freedom from prostitution' social ad campaign

05
HS PINS 'TOTALLY AGAINST GRAPHIC DESIGN'
Self-promotional pins

06
Greenfly 2004
Concert poster, in collaboration with 'Afide Sonoro'

07
Pedrho
Brand image and concept design for an Italian fashion company

08–09
Beauty + Chinagirl 1
HS desktop wallpapers

115

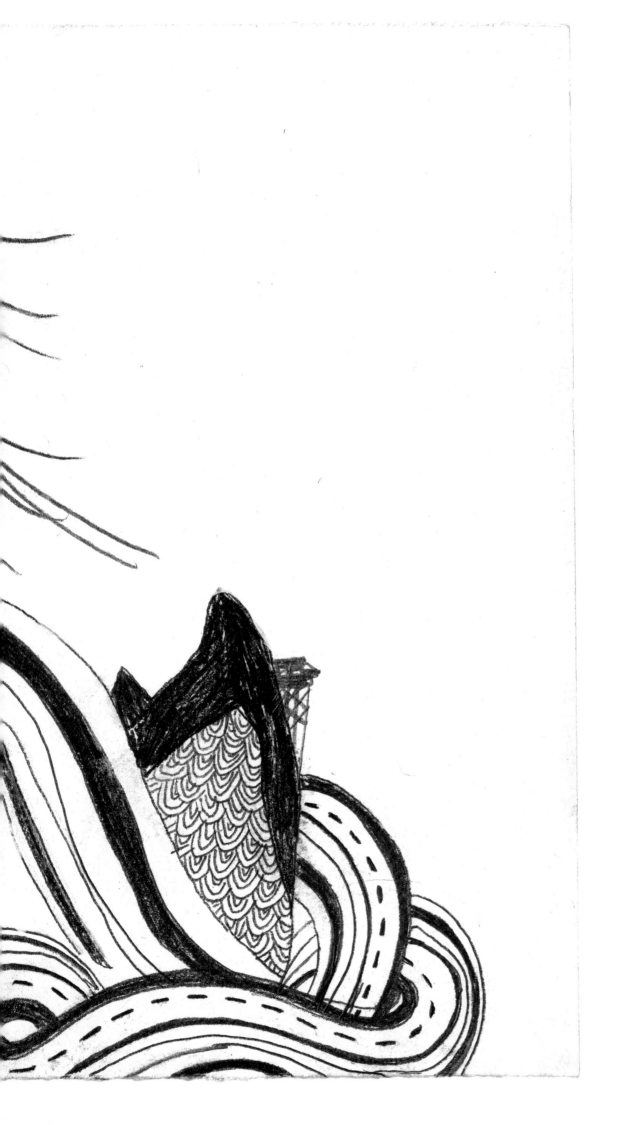

**Prediction Transmission From
Across the Bosporous,
Atlantic and Other Bodies**
2004

A heavy thaw swept in and let things swim again.
It was all early, boisterous, unexpected and late.
Along with it came a prediction transmission
from across the Bosporous, Atlantic other bodies.
If this time machine starts working a stranger has
thrown his last stone. Let's not think about that
now. There came a preface to these heights so let's
just enjoy them.

When asked to name his price,
Ryan Wallace replied: I would do that for you,
I would do that for you.

Ryan Wallace still lives and works in Brooklyn,
New York. Other than riding in a sail plane, he has
been up to more of the same and that is nice. His
work has recently been exhibited in New York, Los
Angeles, San Francisco and Philadelphia. Ryan's
work uses the natural world as starting point in
building narrative worlds with abundant symbolism
and accessible relevance to contemporary
experience. The mostly portrait or landscape
compositions, both obliquely familiar and comforting,
form a piquant counterpoint to the psycho-sexual
and vaguely threatening narratives unfolding in the
pictures. Wallace's narratives remain familiar despite
the intensely personal meanings contained in the
work. Inviting the viewer into his world, sharing with
us the tiny details that form his identity, and revealing
our understanding of how much we have in common.

ryan@ryanmwallace.com
www.ryanmwallace.com

00

01

02

03

04

05

06

07

08

Daniel Eatock
Timothy Evans
Flávia Müller Medeiros
Naoko Sato

following pages [126-129]

Bubble Gum
Bubble Blowing
Self-portrait
08.2004

One camera, one tripod, one cable
release. One box of bubble gum.
Floor marked with where to stand.
Roll up, roll up, do you want to
be in Graphic Magazine? Biggest
bubble printed first, smallest last.
Got to get the timing right! Have a
go, 20p a pop.

126

The long record for colours
2004

I think the most important thing is the imagination. To me, imagination can be thought of as where the future is. I want the work to have a fantasy immediacy that is sexual and to also have a quality that is like pleasure. In my work, I usually combine elements of colour and figure into an image, such as unexpected motif. It is that creation of new aesthetic form that appeals to me.

When asked to name his price, Akinori Shimodaira replied: I enjoy making. For example, making a painting gives me great satisfaction. I know money is very important in society. But I do not have to believe something just for money to influence us.

Born in Tokyo in 1973, B.F.A., Zokei art university, Tokyo, 1995–1999, specializing in sculpture. After graduating from university, between 1998–2001 I started to make art work that was about creating an imaginary man by using writings, objects and music, and sculpting in peoples' minds. Three years ago, I became a freelance designer for the web, magazines and advertising, and started drawing graphic art at the same time.

shimo@murgraph.com
www.murgraph.com

00

01

04

03

05

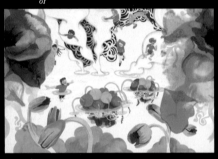

02

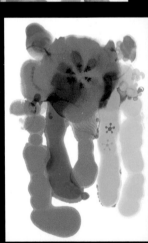

07

08

06

07
Opening or Closing
Illustrations for BEAMS-T and TV program
'Orange days'

00
Akinori Shimodaira

01–02
The Fountain Of Milk
Illustrations for Hong Kong magazine 'CREAM'
based on the theme 'food and eating'

03
Untitled
Illustration for 'Hitoto-shi'

04–06
Untitled
Illustrations for the magazine 'NeoMu', issue 7

08
The New World
Illustration and typeface for Japanese magazine
'CMJ Japan'

Born Stockton-Upon-Tees October 1977 in good health. Moved down south in 1996. Started work at Explosive Design in 1999. Appointed as designer and made responsible for re-design of Sleazenation in 2000. Health takes a turn for the worse. Appointed Art Director in 2002. Left to start freelance business in 2003. Health improves. Work follows for Virgin, BBC, Diabolical Liberties, ICA, Time Out, 679, London Records. Launched Full Moon Empty Sports Bag with co-publishers Ian Allison and Steve Cotton, which soon becomes the only magazine worth reading in London. Planning a book for 2006.

fullmoon@onetel.net
www.utan.co.uk

When asked to name his price,
Patrick Duffy replied: 30 pieces of silver and a pint of Guinness.

Money raises conflicting desires. We want the new product, yet at the same time we want to escape the cycle, stop the mortgage, stop being a calculator. These dual emotions are the basis for this work.

00

01

02

03

04
05

06

07

08

00
Patrick Duffy and his dad, Thomas Duffy

01
Full Moon Empty Sports Bag
Independent magazine, co-published with Ian Allison and Steve Cotton. Spread from issue No.5

02
Diabolical Liberties
Brochure cover, using a butterfly motif to counter Diabolical's reputation as gritty street-media types

03
Jesus Saves, Satan Spends
Poster

04
No Days Off
Tattoo

05
Vote 2004
Poster designed to put pressure on the goverment to call for a referendum on the European Constitution (it worked)

06
Sleazenation
Photography by Jamil GS. Packaged in clear bag with black overprinting

07
Whitey
Album sleeve
Paintings by Chris Graham

08
Fuck Sleep
Pillowcases

The Problem of Leisure; what to do for Pleasure?

Inspired by Natural's Not In It
by Gang Of Four

I do love a new purchase

| Your new easy life | | How can you lose? | One day only | Must end | I can't afford this | I want | I need | Built-in obsolecence | Not included | Offer | Bid now | 0% interest |

| Starts tomorrow | Don't miss out | Buy me | Can't miss | 33% off | Guaranteed | 50% extra free | Brand new | **A market of the senses** 5676-01/11/3848_1:1 | | Free | Win | You must claim |

| The right choice | For successful living | The real thing | You're worth it | Buy one get one | You look nice | Cash | I'm quite partial | Director's cut | New | Debit | Have | Own |

| Pragmatism | Yes please | But you said | Maybe it's | You want | Have a nice day | Now with extra | Credit | Bonus tracks | Looking good | Change your life | Hurry | Don't hesitate |

| Extra power | 3 times shinier | Lifetime | Makes sense | Not idealism | Superior | No thank you | Can I help you? | Come again | Enter your password | Sort code | **Dream of the perfect life** 687-77-644/0/0/0/8763_1:3 Satisfaction guaranteed! |

| No rinse | Stains vanish | Fantastic | Remorse | Hate everything | Love | Death | Renewal | Spiralling | Finance | Economy | Never ending | Monday |

| Terms & conditions | Mortgage | Gifts could be yours | Loss | Destruction | Aquisitions | **Economic circumstances** 687-77-644/0/0/0/8763_1:2 All your dreams come true | | Necessary | At low prices | Pay now | Pay later | Shopaholic |

| Liar | Every little thing | Vordaman | Truth | Stupid | Pleasure | You can't measure | This season | Yesterday | Interiors | Dream home | Less is less | B.O.G.O.F |

| Heat | I forgot | I didn't mean to | I thought | You were right | Can't won't stop | Sure thing | Newly wed | Essential | **The body is good business** 687-77-644/0/0/0/8763_1:4 Your home at risk if you do not keep up repayments on your motgage | | You are important | Kill |

| Sponsored by | Jackpot | Proudly presents | Fourteen new styles | The new | All this week | If you want | You will be | No days off | Not enough | Silent | Now with more | Converted barn |

| In association with | Chip protection | Windfall | Contains new | Hurt me | You will experience | What everyone wants | Sharks | Premium | Studio space | Fresh | Permanent | Hesitation |

| This is it | Amen | **So I maintain the interest** 385/44/-063/44977/5/4/0_1:5 We want you to be happy | | 50% tastier | Navigation | Gestalt | No more odours | Applicator | Fun | Guilt | Whiter | Divorce |

| Sale | Sparkles like | Comfort | Erosion | I see you | Empty and frantic | You knew all along | Money can't buy | Convenience | Dissolution | Schedule | Pocket full of | No way out |

I don't vote Labour or Tory cos I want money and they don't give me money_Shaun Ryder

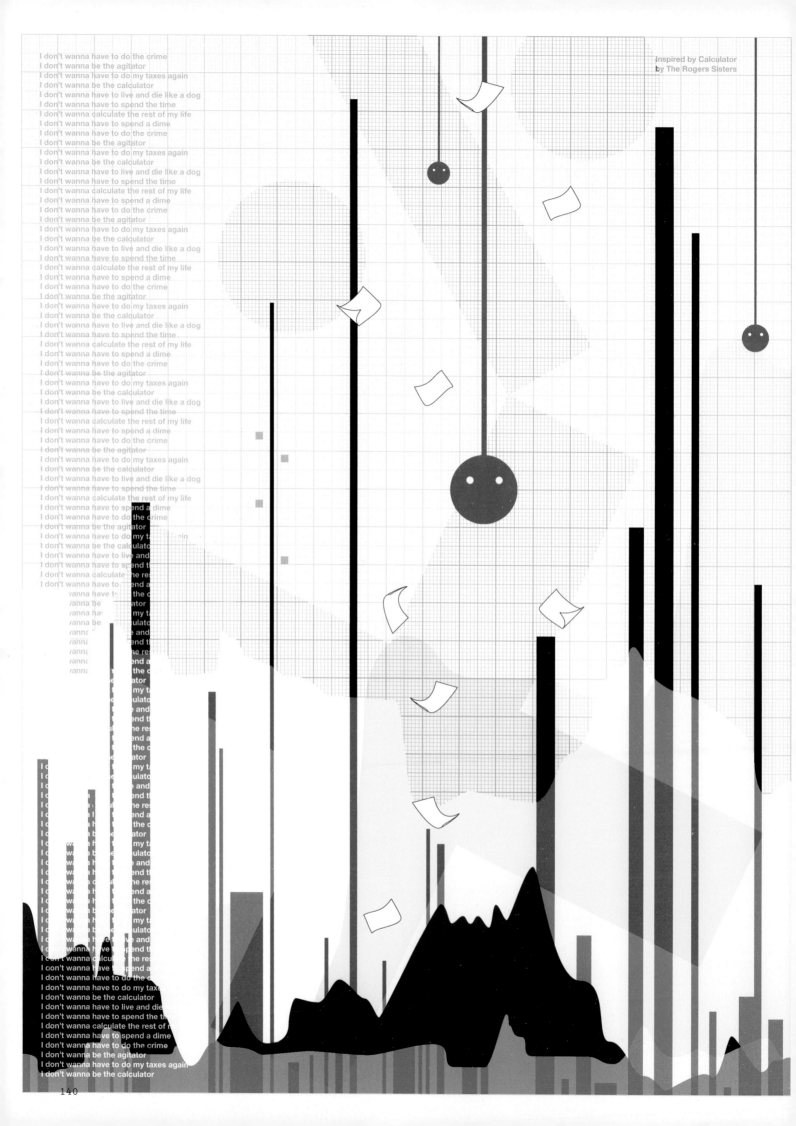

I don't wanna have to do the crime
I don't wanna be the agitator
I don't wanna have to do my taxes again
I don't wanna be the calculator
I don't wanna have to live and die like a dog
I don't wanna have to spend the time
I don't wanna calculate the rest of my life
I don't wanna have to spend a dime
I don't wanna have to do the crime
I don't wanna be the agitator
I don't wanna have to do my taxes again
I don't wanna be the calculator
I don't wanna have to live and die like a dog
I don't wanna have to spend the time
I don't wanna calculate the rest of my life
I don't wanna have to spend a dime
I don't wanna have to do the crime
I don't wanna be the agitator
I don't wanna have to do my taxes again
I don't wanna be the calculator
I don't wanna have to live and die like a dog
I don't wanna have to spend the time
I don't wanna calculate the rest of my life
I don't wanna have to spend a dime
I don't wanna have to do the crime
I don't wanna be the agitator
I don't wanna have to do my taxes again
I don't wanna be the calculator
I don't wanna have to live and die like a dog
I don't wanna have to spend the time
I don't wanna calculate the rest of my life
I don't wanna have to spend a dime
I don't wanna have to do the crime
I don't wanna be the agitator
I don't wanna have to do my taxes again
I don't wanna be the calculator
I don't wanna have to live and die like a dog
I don't wanna have to spend the time
I don't wanna calculate the rest of my life
I don't wanna have to spend a dime
I don't wanna have to do the crime
I don't wanna be the agitator
I don't wanna have to do my taxes again
I don't wanna be the calculator
I don't wanna have to live and die like a dog
I don't wanna have to spend the time
I don't wanna calculate the rest of my life
I don't wanna have to spend a dime
I don't wanna have to do the crime
I don't wanna be the agitator

Listen to what I'm going to tell you now...

Can I have your attention please? Because you're talking about, what, you're talking about bitching about that sale you shot, some son of a bitch don't wanna buy land, somebody don't want what you're selling, some broad you're trying to screw, so forth; let's talk about something important. Are they all here? Well I'm going anyway; let's talk about something important. Put. That coffee. Down. Coffee's for closers only. You think I'm fucking with you? I am not fucking with you. I'm here from downtown. I'm here from Mitch & Murray. And I'm here on a mission of mercy. Your name's Levine? You call yourself a salesman you son of a bitch? I don't gotta listen to this shit. You certainly don't pal, because the good news is, you're fired. The bad news is you've got, all of you've got one week to regain your jobs, starting with tonight, starting with tonight's sit. Oh, have I got your attention now? Good. Because we're adding a little something to this month's sales contest; as you all know, first prize is a Cadillac Eldorado, anybody wanna see second prize? Second prize is a set of steak knives. Third prize is you're fired. You get the picture? You laughing now? You got leads. Mitch & Murray paid good money, get their names to sell them. You can't close the leads you're given, you can't close shit, you are shit, hit the bricks pal and beat it because you are going out. The leads are weak. The leads are weak? Fucking leads are weak? You're weak. I've been in this business 15 years. What's your name? Fuck you, that's my name, you know why mister? Because you drove a Hyundai to get here tonight, I drove a $80,000 BMW, that's my name. And your name is you're wanting, and you can't play in the man's game, you can't close them? Then go home and tell your wife your troubles. Because only one thing counts in this life: get them to sign on the line which is dotted. You hear me you fucking faggots? A, B, C. A, Always, B, Be, C, Closing. Always be closing. Always be closing. A. I. D. A. Attention, Interest, Decision, Action. Attention: do I have your attention? Interest: are you interested, I know you are because it's fuck or walk, you close or you hit the bricks. Decision: have you made your decision for Christ? And Action. A. I. D. A. Get out there, you've got the prospects coming in, you think they came in to get out of the rain? A guy don't walk on the lot lest he wants to buy. They're sitting out there waiting to give you their money. Are you gonna take it? Are you man enough to take it? What's the problem pal, you, Moss. You see this watch? You see this watch? That watch cost more than your car. I made $980,000 last year, how much did you make? See, that's who I am... and you're nothing. Nice guy? I don't give a shit. Good father? Fuck you, go home and play with your kids. You wanna work here? Close... David Mamet, Glengarry Glen Ross

Hi, my name's Patrick Duffy and I'm calling from Full Moon Empty Sports Bag magazine; can I speak to (blank) please? Full Moon Empty Sports Bag magazine. No, we're not a sports magazine, we're a free magazine distributed around London and... no, FULL MOON. Full Moon, yes. Empty Sports Bag. Full Moon Empty Sports Bag, that's right. Yes, it is an unusual name for a magazine, I suppose. Anyway, I was trying to get through to (blank) regarding advertising in our next issue; we're currently booking ads and we thought this would be an excellent opportunity for... yes, we do carry advertising. Yes, I did say it was free, but it's not free to print. Anyway, can I please speak to (blank)? Thank you... Hi there, how you doing? Good, good. So, I'm calling from Full Moon Empty Sports Bag magazine, my names Patrick Duffy and I was told you were the person to talk to... sorry? Full Moon Empty Sports Bag. It's a magazine, yes, and I'm calling regarding advertising in our... yes, Full Moon. Full–Moon–Empty–Sports–Bag–magazine. No, we're not a sports magazine, we're an arts-based free magazine and we're looking to place advertisements in our next issue. Well, we publish you might be interested in placing an ad with us, we distribute 20,000 copies all over London and we've attracted a loyal following and... right... well, we publish poetry, short fiction, journalism, photography... well, in the last issue we had a story about a killer who slits another man's throat with a box-cutter in a public toilet, another one where one man severs another man's head with an axe, a real-life account of a night on the game from a girl who works the streets of Whitechapel, an essay on whether or not suicide in art is a good idea and some astrology by Theodor Weisengrunde Adorno. Previous to that we have had articles on diahorrea, make-up wearing paedophiles, one armed men cutting their own throats, assisted suicide web sites, warlocks, weightlifting, Tarot cards, idiotic reasons for parenthood, Antonin Artaud, shagging Mickey Mouse, real-life vampires, cottaging, Scottish casuals committing murder whilst fucked up on jellies, Japanese teenagers poisoning their parents, Kylie, pregnant, tattooed and high on crack with raging herpes and anal thrush, rent boys, instructions on how to launder drug money, joyriding, fruit machines, the corruption of the Vatican, polyamory, recruitment techniques of the Four Horsemen of the Apocalypse, naïve set theory and the impact of Russell's Paradox, the continuing diary of a questionably sane man and poems on everything from crystal meth addicts to dead drunks crawling with beetles to the Hofmeister bear to innocent punters picking glass out of their faces after an assault by a vicious barmaid. OK... right... so you don't think the Early Learning Centre would be interested. Well, if you change your mind...

KO MMIV

Kevin Devine

King of the Mountain
05.11.2004

there are no more races to be run /
there are no numbers left to be won /
everybody's down, we pulled each other down /
there never was a truth to be found
'Styrofoam', Fugazi 1990

This series of drawings is about social values
and moral judgement. It is an account of a
turning point, a transfer of power. It is also
about chaos and lack of control, violence,
anger, and frustration. It is about man, and his
amazing ability to destroy himself. The drawings
are entitled (in order): The Tower, King of the
Mountain, God, Purgatory.

When asked to name his price,
Kevin Devine replied: gimme a dollar

I was raised by wolves in a den of anarchists
and social misfits. Early on, this pack made a pact;
we committed to a life subverting conventional
behaviour and mainstream thought. My surrogate
family and I will forever move as a force of
calculated recklessness, struggling past the
mundane, creating images that invoke new thoughts
and pushing toward the discoveries that change the
world around us.

I love life. Art empowers me. I look to the past
for education, embrace today as if my last and look
toward tomorrow with great optimism. I also love:
Kansas City, Brooklyn, the LFCrew, the Daggers
clique, and my family.

Kevin Devine makes stylized marks on
surfaces. He hustles commercial design under the
alias Supply&Demand.

kevin@kevindevine.com
www.supply-demand.com
www.kevindevine.com

01

02

03

04

05

06

07

08

00
Kevin Devine

01
Untitled
2003

02
ERS, LFC, KC
2002

03
Image for Pulp Magazine. Article entitled
'The Rebel Yell', 2003

04
Lowrider Astrology
2003
Image for EckoRed

05
Illustration, NeoMu, 2004

06
Logo, MTV TRL
2002

07
Untitled
2002

08
Illustration, Arkitip, 2004

Because:
You'll Finally Make Your Mother Proud. You'll Finally Make Your Father Understand What You Actually Do. You'll Finally Avoid Awkward Conversations At Family Gatherings. You'll Finally Be The Envy Of All Your Colleagues and/or Classmates. You'll Finally Look Good In Job Interviews. You'll Finally Have Something To Say To That Girl/Guy You'll Meet In A Crowded Bar. You'll Finally Get The Attention You've Always Craved. And Because Happiness Will Finally *(Finally!)* Be Yours.

MAKE WORK FOR GRAPHIC!

All Unsolicited Submissions Welcome.
graphic@magmabooks.com

OUT NOW!! **DUTCH DESIGN 2004 2005**

WWW.BISPUBLISHERS.NL

I issue
am still
alive #10
We Buy a Carrot with a Potato (1)

İ Am Still Alive is a parasite magazine. Thank you *Graphic* for hosting. Unless otherwise stated, texts and images: åbäke (Patrick Lacey, Benjamin Reichen, Kajsa Ståhl and Maki Suzuki)
Back issues:
#1 in *Rebel Magazine* 2, automne hiver 2001–2, insert poster p. 50 (Fr)
#2 in *Super, Welcome to Graphic Wonderland*, Thomas Bruggisser and Michel Fries, 2003 İSBN 3-89955-005-6 (Ch)
#3 in *Communication What?*, Ma Edizioni, pp. 120–7, 2002 (İ)
#4 in *İDEA* 297, 2003 pp. 99–114 (Jp)
#5 in *Sport and Street*, April 2003 (İ)
#6 in *Sugo* 0, Ma Edizioni, pp. 16–25, 2003 (İ)
#7 in *idn*:2003:three:volume 10:number 3: flight of fancy ii special insert (HK)
#8 in *Sugo* 1, Ma Edizioni, pp. 112–9, 2004 (İ)
#9 in *A Magazine* 1, Flanders Fashion İnstitute, 2004 İSBN 90-77745-01-7, pp.75–80 (B)

Autumn 2004 in London,

åbäke: *Hi, we had a question. How much would you charge for the design of a book for an artist, A4-ish, 120 pages, mainly black and white… and who do you think should pay? By the way, an editor who comes quite late in the equation will distribute it in Europe. He will get 200 of the publication as some kind of payment, İ guess. Although the whole production is paid by the Arts Council and some money from a Dutch foundation.*

James Goggin: *Well, it depends but it seems something like £3000 to £4000 could be fair.*

å: *Actually, we're asking but there is no money for us. İt got lost somewhere in the process. We still want to do it and we have declined the proposal by the artist to pay from her pocket, which felt unsuitable, or wrong. Right now, we're talking about having our name next to the sponsors, which can be an interesting way to credit our work but let's face it, it won't pay the rent. The other option is to have*

more editorial input over the publication although, come to think of it, this doesn't and shouldn't relate to money.
JG: *I always thought graphic design is probably one of the only field where we'd work more to get less money.*

A current credit card advertisement claims *There are some things money can't buy. For everything else there's ****erCard.*
We are not against the monetary system as such. Our long-term plan is to eradicate it from our immediate surroundings, neighbourhood, small little world. The following series of things we did respond to the accepted templates of conventional work but they offer value in other currencies than hardcore cash.

1/ Where we insisted on doing more than asked.
Death Race 2003, A Friendly Sandpit Race
 A collaboration with artist Shane Bradford and M+R *place to fill:*

Below: How to use the invite-flyer as a record form which will accompany the artwork in the vending machine boxes and function like a catalogue text.

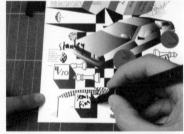

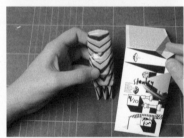

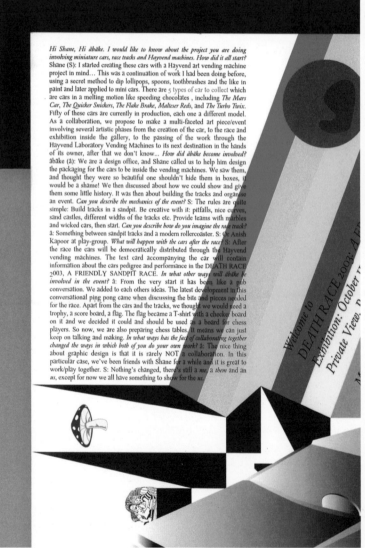

Hi Shane, Hi àbäke. I would like to know about the project you are doing involving miniature cars, race tracks and Hayvend machines. How did it all start? Shane (S): I started creating these cars with a Hayvend art vending machine project in mind... This was a continuation of work I had been doing before, using a secret method to dip lollipops, spoons, toothbrushes and the like in paint and later applied to mini cars. There are 5 types of car to collect which are cars in a melting motion like speeding chocolates , including *The Mars Car, The Quicker Snickers, The Flake Brake, Malteser Reds,* and *The Turbo Twix.* Fifty of these cars are currently in production, each one a different model. As a collaboration, we propose to make a multi-faceted art piece/event involving several artistic phases from the creation of the car, to the race and exhibition inside the gallery, to the passing of the work through the Hayvend Laboratory Vending Machines to its next destination in the hands of its owner, after that we don't know... *How did àbäke become involved?* àbäke (à): We are a design office, and Shane called us to help him design the packaging for the cars to be inside the vending machines. We saw them, and thought they were so beautiful one shouldn't hide them in boxes, it would be a shame! We then discussed about how we could show and give them some little history. It was then about building the tracks and organise an event. *Can you describe the mechanics of the event?* S: The rules are quite simple: Build tracks in a sandpit. Be creative with it: pitfalls, nice curves, sand castles, different widths of the tracks etc. Provide teams with marbles and wicked cars, then start. *Can you describe how do you imagine the race track?* à: Something between sandpit tracks and a modern rollercoaster. S: Or Anish Kapoor at play-group. *What will happen with the cars after the race?* S: After the race the cars will be democratically distributed through the Hayvend vending machines. The text card accompanying the car will contain information about the cars pedigree and performance in the DEATH RACE 2003, A FRIENDLY SANDPIT RACE. *In what other ways will àbäke be involved in the event?* à: From the very start it has been like a pub conversation. We added to each others ideas. The latest development in this conversational ping pong came when discussing the bits and pieces needed for the race. Apart from the cars and the tracks, we thought we would need a trophy, a score board, a flag. The flag became a T-shirt with a checker board on it and we decided it could and should be used as a board for chess players. So now, we are also preparing chess tables. It means we can just keep on talking and making. *In what ways has the fact of collaborating together changed the ways in which both of you do your own work?* à: The nice thing about graphic design is that it is rarely NOT a collaboration. In this particular case, we've been friends with Shane for a while and it is great to work/play together. S: Nothing's changed, there's still a *me,* a *them* and an *us*, except for now we all have something to show for the *us.*

Welcome to
DEATH RACE 2003: A FR
Exhibition: October 1
Private View: N

A ton of sand was barely enough. At the end of the show, the whole circuit got moved to another space. An accidental chess T-shirt competition happened a few months later on a train in Singapore (bottom).

After the *Death Race* experience, we have worked on several occasions with Shane. His latest venture, a touring exhibition called *Arcade* started, for us, as a leaflet-catalogue-job turned into a more interesting experience involving a car and architect Shumon basar. Please read the text—set in Eurovetica, in which accents are literally emphasized—on the previous page for an account of a special journey, originally printed on the back of the poster announcing the event (reduced and reproduced on the next page).

2/ Where we want less money and the necessity of luxury.
We remember from primary school and math lessons the teacher would generally explain why one cannot add carrots and potatoes, whereas it is possible to add, substract, multiply or divide numbers. Money sort of works like that, providing a middle ground, a system by which different things with different values can be measured to and exchanged. Could we cut the middle man out of the equation? Can we rent a flat in exchange of a typeface? We sell 'graphic design' but also use it as a merchandise to barter. Ultimately we are talking about landlords, farmers, plumbers etc. with a need for our so-called expertise and willingness to exchange skills or possessions (please contact this publication if interested).

Who doesn't want to travel?
We have not seen a CV for a long time, especially our own but it used to be common practice to write down that one likes to read, go to the movies or travel. In our opinion, this should only be mentioned if

PLEASURE RIDE
Shumon Basar
Shane Bradford
Åblikе

Sept 7th, 2004

It is uncharacteristically sunny. Shane Bradford, Patrick Lacey and Shumon Basar meet at the Architectural Association, in Bedford Square: a little patch of Georgian loveliness, with a well kempt garden at the centre. But it's a patch that is private. Look, don't enter. That is a law one finds in many places in London. Envy, covet, but don't think about coming in unless you are the right sort. By coincidence, isn't this also the social logic of the Modern gallery space, those stern palaces of white opulence and almost nothingness? From the outside, modern art declares itself to be above the chaff of the everyday world. Concordantly, it is, to some, distanced and intimidating. Åblikе says:

All galleries are a kind of shop.

Shane confesses that:

I have no anxiety about selling my work. Sales pay for progress.

Someone that made a career out of other peoples' anxieties was Sigmund Freud. He helpfully pointed out that we always want what we ultimately can not have. That seeing and wanting are intimately linked. That what you want is the image behind the image. And that can never be accessed, satiated or realized. Is that why we never stop seeing? If we stopped wanting to see, we'd stop wanting. All art unconsciously knows this and trades off it.

Freud's unlikely cohort in revolutionising the 20th century was arguably Karl Marx. Marx is buried at Highgate cemetery, in North London. Shane, Åblikе and I decide to visit his grave. We drive up in Shane's car.

The idea of using the car as a one day office was that we could talk a bit about London and how specific places had some relationship to what Shane does, on our way there. When we arrived we would photograph Shane's drip objects in these different locations.

The placement of the work around London as a means of connecting it to its origins is a great idea and I would have liked to see how much the object responded to the location. The idea of taking art out of the scary white cube gallery space and situating it outside feels very liberating, for the work itself and the person looking at it. But as I said to you before it might have been a little odd in that no one piece of work relates directly to a specific location, the idea is more abstract.

I think that the proposed route was quite a good one, but perhaps because of time, or necessity we ended back in the artist's studio after visiting Marx in Hampstead. We ended up having quite a conventional / formal artist writer discussion. The idea of the car being a vehicle for discussion broke down.

'Breakdown' is the name of Michael Landy's infamous artwork where he destroyed everything he owned in a disused department store on Oxford Street. One might say that Landy's act was retro-Marxist in obliterating the relationship between a person, their material belongings and their identity. Shane loves London, dearly. But he doesn't like the way that its pyrotechnical brilliance is commercially driven and commercially responsive.

On the one hand I love all the lights and the billboards and urban retail detritus, but am frustrated that the main part of its function is commercial. [My] work takes on the city's aesthetic but reworks the content to be something more relevant to my experience.

Is Shane also a retro-Marxist? I don't think so. But some of his gnawing reservations on contemporary life hover closely to what would once have been called a Marxist critique. However, we're so passed labels like that now. Marx's grave, adorned by a beguiling votive Canadian flag, is good as dead. It isn't that artists are necessarily less politicised than before.

They just subsume their politics in a wayward and personal aesthetics. Shane's reasons for making ARCADE reveal a curiosity sparked by the world directly around him.

ARCADE is meant to reflect these things: its most obvious connections being 'shopping arcade' and 'amusement arcade'. Both are a kind of metaphor for the city: at night the city lights up with multi-coloured flashing signs, street lights and displays, most of which are selling or telling you something, advertising their information and enticing you with colour and light like an electric flower. Sometimes the city looks like a pinball machine or a slot machine, urging you with its light displays to come and play it. All this is linked to retail and commercial exchange; shopping, buying, selling, winning, losing, being up on your luck, and being down on your luck, this is the traditional story of the city.

In Shane's paint splattered studio, one finds a menagerie of objects that have undergone his customary dripping process. The colours are a riot of fruity giddiness he says is a derivation of his formative years in sun drenched California. With those kinds of surroundings, a painter mother and sculptor father, was Shane destined to be an artist? Well, no. He has arrived at what he does relatively late, after playing in an art-rock band called Metronome that scowled and screamed and was loved and hated equally by family, friends and fans. Maybe being an artist allows him to fulfil his Utopian impulses to change the world into a world he loves?

Yes, but the word Utopian suggests to me that I would do it for the sake of Utopia itself, that I was in it to create a better society but that's not it at all...I'm not a politician. The satisfaction from making the work comes from a selfish desire to feel special. I don't think I'm special because I make art, but art does make me feel special.

This much is true. Dipping objects over time in cans of household paint is mildly compulsive behaviour, like the woman who couldn't get down her stairs because she would need to make sure all the fibres were lined up in the same direction for her peace of mind. Shane's now recognizable dipped objects signify at a number of communicative levels: as edible sweets, as the painterly macho drip of an abstract expressionist or paint fossils that encase real objects in a thick, glutinous scaleless substance. The newer stuff also works with existing things, but is the pursuit of a boffin-like scientist who tinkers disassembles and re-assembles.

By changing, or re-structuring something like a television set, manipulating it into something I like better, in the broadest sense, I am creating an individual identity for myself in the face of mass production and mass opinion. It is perhaps political in that it is a form of rebellion, but it's a modern form that recognises the futility of opposing the machine and one that seeks only to provide a purpose for myself. Hopefully though on a less narcissistic note it

also encourages original individual expression and tries to persuade the masses that art and 'stuff-that-looks-deeper' is ultimately more fulfilling, more entertaining, and more optimistic than the 5th series of "I'm a Celebrity, Get Me Out of Here"

Shane tells us that he'll keep dipping objects to support the other experiments he does. Is he on to an On Kawara or Joseph Albers formula? Is the deadpan repetition of doing the same (kind of) thing a reactive statement about declaring 'I am alive'? The dips need to be read in relation to the other things emerging from the studio: like the TVs Shane is so enamoured with, his practice switches channels, hops and surfs hoping to find something new or something you already know. Television is shamanistic. It is a lateral landscape of promises. And best of all, television allows you to edit what actually happened, to present it to the world post-production, with the 'fucks' and the 'cunts' all bleeped out. Television, like art, mutates history into idealized forms of eternal remembrance.

Recently I was talking to Elia Gibbs [a London based artist] about this trend for publishing email correspondence... maybe everyone is on their guard now, knowing that it's possible our candid exchanges might end up in one of those 'bookmagazines'. Will anyone sped check? Is it a passing trend?

Patrick has known Shane for a long time now. They share a common virtue which is to be highly suspicious of self-aggrandizement. It's a 'tell it like it is' attitude that, for the most part, remains true to its modest cause. But deep down, I suspect they are as mindful of their legacies as Salvador Dali, Liberace or James Dean:

Shumon and I were having a laugh the other day about how this text can be an opportunity to say what you wish you had said at the time. We all (at least I do) play out fantasies about things we wished we had said and done in order to come to terms with what we actually DID say or do...

On our day driving through London, our car nearly hit an oncoming motorcycle. This is a common occurrence in the city, where everyone is trying to get somewhere in a maddening rush, somehow de-sensitised to the presence of the millions of others on the road. Shane remembers the event: ... Telling the guy to fuck off wasn't the best way of handling the situation. So now the opportunity is there to tell a version where I handle it really well!

For the record, Shane is a sensitive and considerate driver. Or that's what this version of our day out is claiming. Walter Benjamin said he was interested in history in so far as it was "the politics of the present". If Shane Bradford makes art to feel special or to change the world by creating things, images, surfaces and memento, then he is involved in altering how the rest of us see the past by engaging with the present. Our memories are a fuzzy domain of half-remembered truths and invented fictions. Shane Bradford makes art to pleasure himself. And that is just being honest. Pleasure is deeply deep, and is a key to working out why any of us do what we do. Paint, screens, white noise and rainbows are forms of pleasure. Pleasure is tragedy, comedy, commerce, desire, hurt, selfishness and altruism. And I suspect Shane knows this all too well.

Arcade poster, front and back reproduced in various reductions, according to grid, legibility and taste concerns

'Arcade'	Stiftelsen 3,14 Hordaland	M.K. Ciurlionis National	M+R
Shane Bradford	International Art Gallery	Museum of Art	place to fill
Curated by Mark thompson	Bergen, Norway 2004	Kaunas, Lithuania 2005	London, UK 2005

design och fotografi av Åblikе

one doesn't like any of these cliché hobbies. In this sense, we feel ourselves very normal in appreciating exotic places, combined with the celebratory event birthdays are (Please refer to *I am still Alive* #4 and #7 for previous occurences). One needs a combination of luck, persuasion and the will to provoke it, the latter being something we need to develop a bit more. From experience, May and November are better for conference/workshop related events we are invited to. Luck plays a mysterious but important role as some events, like the Idn *My Favourite Conference* (2004) in Singapore or the mu.dac *Sooo rational!* talk in Lausanne (2003) were respectively held on the same dates as Patrick and Kajsa's birthdays. Other trips are to be negotiated and the dates for the workshop we organised at Fabrica in Treviso were simply decided because of our little ritualistic obsession. As well as enjoying local food and festivities, the travelling itself gives us plenty of opportunity to make things.

Hotel 17, by Zongamin, a 12 inch release on Kitsuné is a double A-side, which means it has another title, subjectively equal in quality on its other side.
www.kitsune.fr

How many birds can one kill with a single stone?

The Happy Birthday (Kajsa 2003) in Lausanne.
François Rappo, graphic designer and typographer invited GTF, Norm and ourselves for an evening of talks called *Sooo rational!*. François had told us it had something to do with Josef Muller-Brockman's *The Graphic Artist and His Design Problems*, which we had not read at the time. Interestingly, we found positive echoes in the publication with what had driven us to 'push our birthdays' forward within our work. Later that night, we thought it relevant to take advantage of the unusual place and context by setting an impromptu photoshoot for the record sleeve of a release from our own small label (Kitsuné). The 12 inch vynil sleeve on Zongamin's *Hotel 17* photographically records a timid amateur rock'n roll moment: a carefully trashed hotel room in switzerland which we obviously cleaned and left immaculate.

The Happy Birthday (Patrick 2004) in Singapore.
Laurence Ng and his team at İdn magazine welcomed us and more than a dozen design groups to take part in a warehouse design conference in Singapour. In response to which we designed a souvenir T-shirt for the visitors. We just scrambled the letters of the 'official design', transforming a somewhat obscure slogan (*My Favourite Conference 2004 Hook on your Favourites*) into an equally strange anagram. The name of the talkers printed in the back were treated in the same way (Delaware became Lewd Area), resulting in total gibberish accentuating the fact it is only fully understandable by someone who had been there. A Souvenir which becomes complete with the subjective memory of the owner.

The Happy Birthday (Kajsa 2004) in Venice.
The invitation came from Giorgio Camuffo, a big-hearted graphic designer who was born and works in Venice and Omar Vulpinari, head of Communication at Fabrica. The workshop we held at the 'school' will be the subject of a coming issue of *I am still Alive.* In addition to this, Giorgio let us use the ground floor of his beautiful studio in the middle of the water city to show some recent and Venice-related projects. In commemoration of our friendship, we produced a 'handshake' t-shirt called *We Connect*. For the opening of the show, furniture designer Martino Gamper flew especially from London to serve a rather successful series of soup (raddichio, onion or pumpkin). For our last evening, we invited him to our favourite restaurant: *Al Mascaron*. Martino has never been shy to acquaint with strangers and got to chat to the manager/waiter of the place about what we 'do' for a big part of the dinner. A discussion leading to another, Martino made us promise to send a Venice t-shirt to Mario. When he finally brought the bill, he gave us a more than generous discount. One of us remarked we had somehow sold a t-shirt for 75 euro, a rather good price.

As a continuation of this tradition, we offer our services to people from different countries, around the 11th of January, 14th of May, 10th of August and 26th of November of whichever year in the future. This text is to be continued.

Top to bottom: original poster artwork by İdn, the anagram T-shirt, front and back

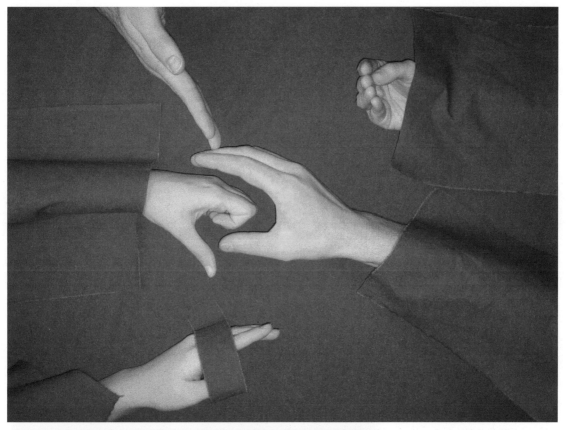

Clockwise from top: the image announcing a workshop at Fabrica and an exhibition in Venice, the business card from *Al Mascaron* (an advertisement) and the '75 euro' t-shirt

Next page: 'R' in our on-going series of *The Slow Alphabet*

2K
Y GINGHAM

LET'S
SHARE.

Artwork by Geoff McFetridge

Norrath is a young country; it was formed on March 16th, 1999. It has a small population, around 60,000, and while hardly a rich country its GNP per capita is US$2,266, enough to make it the 77th richest country in the world – richer than India and China, and roughly equal to Russia. Where Norrath differs from these countries, however, is that it is an entirely virtual world; a videogame construct.

Insert Coin(s)

Text by Samuel Baker

Economist Edward Castronova produced a paper on the subject of market economics in virtual worlds (VWs) in December 2001, focusing primarily on Norrath. Norrath is the setting for events in Sony Online Entertainment's MMORPG (massively multiplayer online role-playing game), EverQuest. At the time of the report, Castronova's figures showed roughly 400,000 active accounts, with a population of around 60,000 players present at any one time, split between a number of servers (each server hosts a slightly different version of Norrath, without any transfer of information or wealth between them yet all existing simultaneously). Around 93,000 people spend more time in Norrath per week than they do working for pay — and despite paying subscription fees, time spent in Norrath is in fact profitable in real financial terms. Items and currency, merely portions of computer code in a system, are bought and sold for 'real-world' currency in privately arranged transactions or on internet auction sites. Indeed, around 20% of EverQuest players consider themselves residents, partially earning a living there and merely 'commuting to Earth'. For these, Castronova calculated that an hour spent in Norrath yields 'utility worth $14.15' — considerably more money than is outlayed per month in subscription fees. And if a user spends 80 hours or so a week in Norrath, their income equates to more than $12,000 a year; the poverty line in the US is $8,794. It is feasible — albeit unlikely — that people actually live and work in Norrath.

So is Norrath in fact a real country? If a populated space produces a demonstrable GNP, and people consider themselves citizens, why not? Quite apart from the monster-slaying and looting, there have been in-game marriages (often in addition to a ceremony on Earth) and funerals. Much of the game is resolutely social, with many players acting as merchants or innkeepers in addition to more traditional adventuring roles. And recent developments in other games seem to support the idea that these worlds are considerably more complex social systems than is at first apparent.

Star Wars Galaxies, a relatively new MMORPG also published by SOE, experienced an unplanned series of

This is my house in Animal Crossing (Nintendo Gamecube). I haven't been playing very long but already I have exerted considerable effort in the pursuit of home improvement. You start with a very small and basic home – this is the next size up. I understand that eventually you can attain a much larger house with a basement. The contents are, from top left to bottom right: a shimansen, which plays the town theme tune when you pluck it (you can change the town theme – I changed it to a portion of the Super Mario theme); an unusual umbrella with Japanese *kanji* on it; a Donkey Kong NES game; a Tennis NES game; a bug-eyed goldfish I caught in the river and decided to keep instead of selling; a simple fern plant; a 'modern' sofa which I don't much like, but which I am yet to find an adequate replacement for; a pool table; a cheap stereo with a single annoying tune (I have yet to acquire other music cassettes); a Christmas tree; a trestle table, on which rests a number of tombola tickets, and my diary.

The wallpaper is a pattern I designed myself at Abel & Mabel's fabric shop. It is a sort of Eley Kishimoto pastiche. The floor is also a pattern of my own design, to look like a dark hardwood floor (very similar to that in my real home). The clothes I am wearing are from another self-made pattern. I prefer these to the other wallpapers, floors and clothes that I have acquired so far in the game.

This is my character in Virtua Fighter 4 Evolution (PlayStation 2). He is the fairly advanced Hunter rank, although that is largely a result of having dropped the game to its Easy setting. As tasks are completed and tournaments won, money is earned and items can be acquired. I have my character dressed mainly in grey, with a silk blindfold, long braided hair, wearing a silver necklace and carrying a silver flute.

This is one of my ACs (Armored Core) in Armored Core 2 (PlayStation 2). It is the standard bipedal configuration and includes the rare Karasawa-Mk2 rifle equipped on the right arm. It is rated at a total of 38791 points with an overall classification of 'Excellent'.

social events when a few unscrupulous players discovered how to duplicate in-game credits — essentially creating forged currency. They produced large quantities of this illegal cash, using it to purchase all the items they could want and flooding the economy (partially aided by a system in SWG which allows a player to 'tip' another player any amount of cash without them actively accepting it). Understandably keen to stamp out this potentially game-ruining practice, SOE started banning the accounts of those it felt were responsible. The problem was, because the forged currency had become so ubiquitous a number of innocent players who had unwittingly received duped credits were also banned — while some known dupers walked free. Complaints flooded in but little appeared to be being done. SOE seemed unwilling or unable to cope with the problem.

Incensed by this injustice, friends of the banned innocents began organising protests, crowding public places and repeatedly demanding that their friends be un-banned. As their servers clogged up with protesters, the game slowing to a crawl, game moderators became increasingly desperate in their measures to control the crowds. Eventually, they resorted to teleporting troublemakers away, sometimes to distant or dangerous areas of the game world, even — allegedly — into space. The events were covered by a few players acting as self-appointed news reporters, taking screenshots and conducting interviews from the scene. This record still exists (intrepid.galaxyforums.com/index.php?showtopic=7190) and is a noteworthy example of the fact that even simple VW systems can create remarkably complex — and Earth-like — social behaviour; sometimes unintentionally.

There are some newer VWs that actively pursue the idea of a world linked to Earth currency, and separated from the fantasy and competition elements that have traditionally formed the bedrock of MMORPGs. Project Entropia is one such VW which, while still incorporating game elements, has its in-game currency linked to the US dollar and encourages the purchase of game items and currency with 'real' money. PE recently made headlines after a public auction was held to sell an in-game island (www.project-entropia.com/Content.ajp?id=1346), complete with a castle, hunting & mining rights, and the rights to sell land lots to in-game developers. The price? 265,000 PED: that's US$26,500.

Another is Second Life (secondlife.com), which finally removes any vestige of traditional game structure and instead becomes a complex 'sandbox' world. Residents can enter the world for a small initial fee, create an avatar and simply live in the VW. They can shop, play games, explore, build items and businesses and generally make their way in this new, parallel world. Highly flexible in-game tools allow the player, with an investment of time and effort, to craft all manner of detailed objects, including vehicles, robots, sculptures, machines and buildings. People have already set up car dealerships, paying real-money rent and selling real-money — yet virtual — automobiles, and there is much talk of real-world franchises opening outlets in the VW, selling virtual reproductions of real-world goods.

But why? What's the appeal of a game world over real life, especially if you still have to pay real money to own expensive things?

Fantasy is obviously a factor — unaided flight

and space travel are both possible in Second Life - as is the ability to create an avatar from scratch, with any physical attributes you so desire, with equal opportunities for all. And if you end up unhappy with the way things go, be it with a bad reputation or few friends, you can always start again from scratch. But one thing common to all successful VWs is the concept of scarcity.

Castronova identifies that early (free) VWs were essentially 'avatar spaces' — anyone with the time and inclination could build quite as much as they wanted. One could create any number of avatars, and bestow them with any number of characteristics and powers. Yet, counter-intuitively, it seems that this is rather less fun than a world in which everything has a price, whether in terms of currency or at the risk of death. And nothing comes for free; one of the most important aspects of a VW is that of society and, in turn, competition. The avatar must work if he or she is to achieve anything of consequence. Castronova states:

> '…people seem to prefer a world with constraints to a world without them. Constraints create the possibility of achievement, and it is the drive to achieve something with the avatar that creates an obsessive interest in her well-being.'

Rewards are nothing without the requisite work. The curious aspect of videogame rewards, however, is that they are by definition intangible. They are transient images on a screen, portions of code representing fictional currency or imaginary items of clothing or weapons. We cannot, as the phrase goes, take it with us. But perhaps that is the point. Castronova again:

> '…since the VWs are inherently social, the achievements are relative: it is not having powerful weapons that really makes a difference in prestige, but in having the most powerful weapons in the world. In a post-industrial society, it is social status, more than anything else, that drives people to work so diligently all their lives. In this respect, VWs are truly a simulacrum of Earth society.'

It could be argued that these rewards, achieved through hard work, without the handicaps of inequality of birth, are at least as real as those in our native world, and considerably more appealing in their meritocratic nature.

Of course, VWs aren't the only show in town. The automated high score table is a piece of videogame language that's older than the medium itself, having originated in pinball machines, but it's a device that's inherent to much videogame design. Numerical quantification of otherwise abstract activity comes naturally to computer systems, and it alters the meaning of human competition from *I beat this guy at that game last time we played* to *I am this much better at that game than he is.* Your social standing is displayed for all the world to see, your numerical worth totted up and indisputable. This is the purest, truest meritocracy, a measure of individual skill and nothing else.

At its highest level, though, it stops being about the numbers in much the same way that, at some point, accruing ever more money becomes practically meaningless. It's possible to simply play the numbers game, to do what you have to do — as long as you have the skill. But to really earn the respect of your peers it all comes back round to artistry, to the reason you started playing in the first place. There might be two ways of earning a particular score on a particular

This is my highscore table for Ikaruga (Nintendo Gamecube). My highscore for normal difficulty & default settings is 7,252,450, reaching chapter 3. I set the score on the 11th September 2003. I can achieve an S rank on the first chapter but do poorly after that. This score is better than any of my immediate friends but very poor compared to an expert player, who might score more than 32,000,000 points.

This is my highscore table for Psyvariar (Revision version, PlayStation 2). My highscore is 26,594,000 (default settings, no continues), reaching area X-B. I set this score on 11th October 2003. It is slightly higher than those of my immediate friends, but poor compared to an expert player. I have returned to the game only once or twice since setting the score, partly because I don't like it as much as other shmups I own, but mainly because my friends stopped playing it and there was no longer a competition between us.

This is my highscore table for Espgaluda (PlayStation 2). My highscore for normal difficulty & default settings is 9,580,540, reaching area 3. I set the score on the 26th July 2004. I have set other scores where I have reached area 4, but improved scoring techniques meant that I scored higher on that run. Much room for improvement here.

– – – – – – – – – – – – – – – – –

Your social standing is displayed for all the world to see, your numerical worth totted up and indisputable

section of a particular game, but one may be workmanlike and formulaic where the other is elegant and creative. It's a level of play that few will ever achieve, but it's there to be appreciated and admired; more so than ever thanks to the proliferation of video capture equipment and the internet. Anyone familiar with Super Monkey Ball cannot fail to be astonished at the efforts of some of the hard-core players (www.ajshakesby.co.uk/smbvids), particularly PackAttack's legendary — and absurdly difficult — Advanced level 11 run.

And the internet is also enabling record-keeping of unprecedented complexity and comprehensiveness. Halo 2 for Xbox (bungie.net/Games/Halo2/) has already been so successful that Microsoft have upwardly revised their Xbox division's profit forecasts solely because of the revenues from it. This success is in large part due to the exceptional scorekeeping system implemented by Bungie, the game's developers. Halo 2 has a strong focus on its online multiplayer modes, tapping into the Xbox Live matchmaking service but going far beyond it by recording every detail of every match — moments after finishing a game, you can log on to Bungie's website and see the names and emblems of the people you were playing with, the type of game, exactly how many times you killed and were killed, how many times you scored a particular objective and so on, right down to precisely how many shots each person fired. It even allows a graphic summary of the game from many different angles, and allows almost all this information to be broadcast as individual RSS feeds. This last feature enables anyone with a bit of coding ability to keep a permanent web database of all the data, and compare and filter it accordingly. The level of detail is mind-boggling — my friends and I all have our data collected into a simple site that one of us set up, where we can endlessly compare our kills-per-death ratios or the number of headshots scored per game, in top-ten indices and pie charts. *Pie charts,* for goodness' sake.

And this, I believe, is one of the main reasons the game has been such a success. With the original Halo, these things also occurred, the magic moments and heroic stories. But they never left the living room. You could tell people about them, sure, but now — now you can *show* them.

And, of course, I'm sure it appeals to the obsessive types in all sorts of new ways. If there was ever a game to obsess over, this is it. But it remains, fundamentally, a social experience. It has work, it has reward, it has social standing and hierarchy and anecdote and empathy and idiots and communication and teamwork. Maybe, though, it is the endless numerical comparison that points toward the future of social structures in videogames; the irrepressible human imperative to acquire, and demonstrate, status amongst one's peers.

* * *

Edward Castronova's paper:
papers.ssrn.com/sol3/papers.cfm?abstract_id=294828
Edward Castronova's homepage:
mypage.iu.edu/~castro/home.html
Gaming Open Market (VW currency exchange):
www.gamingopenmarket.com
IGE (MMORPG goods and currency traders):
www.ige.com

Q&A:
This Is Real Art

How did 'This Is Real Art' come about?

It began by selling signed prints by leading graphic designers online. We had prints by Fuel, Blue Source, Kim Hiorthoy, Julian House and Anthony Burrill. It was reasonably successful, but the most important thing that came out of it was, that we acquired relationships with some really interesting designers and artists.

We were constantly approached by designers looking to sell their work online, and noticed that there were lots of fantastic freelance designers who were capable of doing great work but, because of their fierce desire to remain independent, were missing out on opportunities. Many of them were being regularly approached by ad agencies, but the discussions rarely came to anything because designers, or the sort of designers we were talking to, seemed reluctant to play the games you sometimes have to play with the big agencies.

All the designers wanted to remain autonomous, but it occurred to us that if they could have some support, some sort of structure, then they might do really well. So, we developed the idea of a virtual design company. In other words, a design company that employs no designers, but which has lots of good designers. At present there are three of us, Kate Nielsen, Sarah Withers and myself. We have one full-time in-house designer (Sam Renwick), and we have Adrian Shaughnessy as consultant creative director. All the designers are rostered. It's the way production companies work – directors are on the roster and only work when a job comes in. But no one's done it for graphic design – as far as we can tell.

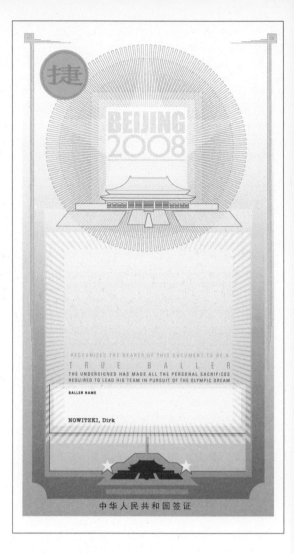

There is a regular feature in one of the British Sunday newspapers where dimly recognisable celebrities, and half-remembered sports-stars are quizzed about their personal finances. Each week the subjects are asked the same set of questions. These include: 'Have you ever been poor?'; 'Are you a saver or a spender?'; 'What is the most lucrative thing you've ever done?' Reading the mildly-boastful answers is a sort of financial voyeurism: the soft porn of personal finance. But there's one question that no one ever gives a straight answer to. The question is this: 'How much did you earn last year?' I've never known anyone to name a figure.

Money

Text by Adrian Shaughnessy

Why the shyness? Are they frightened to state an amount in case a tax inspector is reading the article while munching his or her toast and marmalade? I'd have thought that evasiveness was more likely to attract the attention of a tax official, looking for a celebrity scalp to hang on the wall alongside the pictures of kittens that granite-hearted tax officials hang on their office walls. Asking someone how much they earn is a tricky question. Not many people will give you a straight answer. People will sooner talk about their sexual dysfunctionalism, or tell you their most lurid fantasies, rather than tell you how much they earn. Low earners are more likely to tell you than high-earners. Ask a rich person how much they earn and you are unlikely to get a friendly answer: you will get a pleasanter response if you stick a finger up one of their nostrils and wiggle it from side to side.

For this article, I was going to thumb my nose at financial secretiveness and announce how much money I earned last year. But my nerve has failed me. I just can't bring myself to do it. It's too personal, too revealing. Designers are especially coy on the subject of money. We will happily tell you everything you want to know about one of our projects — what influenced us, how we found our client, how the work was received — but we won't tell you how much we were paid for doing the job. It is clear from reading the glossy design magazines and the polemical design blogs, that money is a taboo subject in graphic design. It is rarely mentioned. One of the few individuals willing to break this financial omerta, is Stefan Sagmeister. In his wonderful and idiosyncratic monograph Made You Look, Sagmeister lists all the fees he earned

It's too personal, too revealing. Designers are especially coy on the subject of money

Above
Ben Drury / This Is Real Art
for Wieden + Kennedy
Nike Visa Stamps

Left
Robert Ryan / This Is Real Art
Museum of Us Exhibition

When was it set up?

We set up the virtual design company in the summer of 2004. It is however, only within the past two or three months that we have gotten a settled roster, and are now starting to get regular work.

Why did you think this was a good idea?

Well, we spotted that there were lots of interesting designers, Kim Hiorthoy is a good example, who have the potential to do really interesting work on a bigger stage, but on their own the chances of achieving this are slim. But, with our project management experience and our ability to put together proposals, pitches, budgets and schedules, all the things that highly creative designers usually hate doing, we think we can allow our designers to stay free but do some heavyweight work.

Adrian Shaughnessy made a big difference when he joined us. He has lots of experience and has dealt with clients of all kinds. He is well known amongst a certain sort of designer, so he has been very important in helping us find the right people to work with, and helping us win some big jobs.

Who were the first artists you worked with?

Ben Drury was a key member. He's like the grand old man of 'This is Real Art.' Kate Nielsen had worked with him on various Mo' Wax projects before 'This is Real Art' started, so there was a strong relationship already in place. Ben is doing some extraordinary things. People who only know him for his Mo' Wax and Dizzie Rascal work will be surprised to see how versatile he is. He has been working for Nike via Wieden + Kennedy in Amsterdam. W+K have been very supportive of 'This is Real Art.' They were amongst the first people we went to see, and they understood what we were trying to do.

Robert Ryan is also a founding member. Rob's paper cut-outs are getting a lot of interest. Liberty's and Japanese Vogue have commissioned work. He has also just done the new album cover for Erasure. We're looking at ways of animating his work. There is a lot of interest in that.

Michael Place was another early member of the roster. Michael approached us, and together we have done some amazing jobs, all of which are currently under wraps, but they will be revealed in the New Year.

What makes 'This is Real Art' different?

It is not about representation. We don't 'represent' the designers on our roster. We 'partner' with them to form a virtual design company. For our clients, working with us should feel like dealing with any good design company, the only difference is we don't employ any of the designers on our roster. We can offer an astonishing array of talent, far more than any conventional design company could hope to.

We don't have contracts. We have a manifesto that is strongly tipped in favour of the designers. Everyone is free to do what he or she wants, to leave when they want, to decide what they do or do not want to do. The only rule is that if a designer agrees to do a job, they have to see it through. I'm sure our manifesto would freak out any lawyer, but it seems to work.

Clients like this way of working. Agencies have been especially supportive. Most of our early work has come from agencies. We've made two films for TBWA with Michael Place, and we've just made one for Fallon. I suppose agencies are not fazed by the idea of a roster. But we've also had a good response from non-agency clients. Channel 4 has been a good client. They really get what we do, they like the diversity.

Another important part of 'This is Real Art' is staging exhibitions. We don't want to become a boring design company. We want to do lots of non-client things. We've held an exhibition of Rob Ryan's work at the Horse Hospital, which was really successful.

> The problem for designers is that we love what we do too much not to care when we are compromised

Right
Build/This Is Real Art
for This Is Real Art
Christmas Card
2004

Far right
Matt Pyke/This Is Real Art
for Fallon
Film

nice advert →

for the various projects he reproduces in his book. This seems an almost heroic gesture on his part. You wouldn't catch one of the big muscle-y, steroid-pumped design groups with chic, air-conditioned offices around the world doing this: their shareholders wouldn't allow it.

At first glance, there seems to be a good reason for financial secretiveness in graphic design. It's a business, after all, and it's highly competitive — so why give our rivals an edge by telling them how much we were paid for a job when there's a chance that one of them will simply ring up our client and offer to do the same job, next time around, for half the fee. But I don't think commercial sensitivity is the main reason for designer's coyness about money. It's got more to do with the psychology, and cultural legacy, of being a designer. Designers are surprisingly high-minded. Vocation is an unfashionable word, but most designers think of their career as vocational — even if not many would use that word. Few designers grow up wanting to be a designer. Until recently, it was rare to see it even listed as a career option in schools. For most of us, design is something we discover by accident — usually in our late teens — and feel inexorably drawn towards it. Money is rarely one of the deciding factors in making up our minds to become a designer.

Once we've made the decision to become a designer, we go to university to study the subject. And after three, sometimes five years, we emerge ready to start work. Then, we experience the cattle prod of reality: we discover that our ideas are brutally compromised by financial and business realities, with the result that even the most pragmatic of designers often feel that their integrity is under assault. This is painful. The problem for designers is that we love what we do too much not to care when we are compromised. It would be much easier if we didn't care. But we do, and it's the reason that we are not well-equipped to deal with the compromises inherent in the act of making money. If you want to make money, you have to have a thick skin, and you can't be too fussy about what you do. It's the reason why there aren't many graphic design millionaires. (There is a tiny handful of robust designer/entrepreneurs who have managed to lodge a six figure sum in their building society saving accounts: but most of them have made their loot by selling their companies to one of the marketing and advertising conglomerates that owns all the big design groups, rather than by being paid for 'doing' graphic design.)

I'm often envious of people who make money. It's not the money I envy (well, I do a bit), rather it's the ease with which they make it. They don't seem to have any impediments, other than the normal cut and thrust of commercial life. Estate agents, used car dealers, lawyers, they don't seem to mind what they sell or who they represent. An estate agent will sell a stone-clad, PVC-windowed, architectural nightmare next to a by-pass, with the same unblinking unctuousness as a house designed by Mies van der Rohe; a used car dealer will happily flog you a gas-guzzling, ozone-destroying, robot-wars-tank; and lawyers represent rapists, crack dealers and gun toting criminals without batting an eyelid (yes, I know there's a sophisticated jurisprudence philosophy at work here, that demands equal representation for all, but you get my drift.)

If only it was so simple in design. If only we didn't care so much about which jobs we do. If only we could turn to our clients and say, smiling warmly, OK, no problem,

Who are you working with now?

We've had two people drop out for various reasons, but this is ok, because it's part of the spirit of the enterprise that everyone is free to stay or go. We only want people who want to stay. We'd never try and persuade someone to stay if they wanted to leave.

So the roster at the time of writing is: Build, Ben Drury, Trevor Jackson, UVA, Rob Ryan, Kim Hiorthoy, Donald Christie and Tom Hingston. We're launching some new names in the New Year.

What makes your artists different?

I'd say it's this idea of independence. They are all ambitious and hard working, but nothing will ever make them give up their autonomy. None of them will ever end up working for a design studio, for example. There also has to be trust between the designers and us. If they don't trust us to help them, it won't work.

They also need to be ambitious. Tom Hingston's a good example. He has a fantastic company. He does really well, winning awards and is always busy, but he wants to move onto bigger projects. He is not interested in selling-out, he just wants to take what he does for record labels, publishers and fashion houses, to a bigger stage.

But it's not just about doing bigger jobs. We will do anything as long as it is interesting, and as long as it has real aesthetic or social worth. We've been talking to Greenpeace, for example. Not with a view to making money, but with a view to creating work that will have social impact.

What do you look for in an artist you might want to include in your roster?

Trust, talent and graft. We're only interested in really talented people, and we're only interested in people who are not frightened by big clients, big projects or hard work. But then I've never met a good designer who wasn't like this.

Is business good?

Better than we thought. We didn't expect much in the first year, but people have been really keen to work with us. I think we need a few groundbreaking jobs under our belt before we can expect lots of work, but it's looking good. We've had to take a larger office, and my guess is, we will grow this year.

What are your goals and plans for the future?

We would like 'This is Real Art' to be seen as the first place clients look for talent. Someone has advised us to charge clients to see the portfolio: I'm not sure we'll ever do that, but the concept is right. We are giving clients access to some remarkable talent, and we are creating a situation where clients are able to work with some marvellous people. Maybe we should charge to show the portfolio. £300 a look, anyone?

*   *   *

www.thisisrealart.com

Taste is a fatal flaw
to possess if you want
to make money.
Designers have to
live with this flaw
in their chromosomes

Above
Kim Hiortoy / This Is Real Art
for Sonic Youth
CD Cover

Left
Robert Ryan / This Is Real Art
for Liberty
**Liberty Shaun Leanne Jewelry
Launch Invitation**

I'll change everything and I'll do it all in red — no problem whatsoever. This is not to say that designers don't like making money, or that they don't think that they should be well-paid for what they do. And it must also be recognised that there are designers who are 'in it for the money' — but they are different; they usually call themselves 'branding consultants' and they don't care what they do, or who they do it for just so long as they can charge a lot of money. Which of course, is the secret of making money. My accountant has been telling me for years: stop being so fussy about who you work for and what you do; just think about the money.

The British designer and art director Peter Saville, an even more quixotic figure than Sagmeister, said in a recent article in The Times (15 Sept 2004): 'The trouble with graphic design today is: when can you believe it? It's not the message of the designer anymore. Every applied artist ends up selling his or her soul at some point. I haven't done it and look at me. People call me one of the most famous designers in the world and I haven't got any money.' It's as if Saville is saying, the more talented you are, the less money you will make. Perhaps what he means is that if you want to do great work — or as he calls it, 'work you can believe in' — you have to forgo financial reward.

But I've never met a designer, at least one who was any good, who didn't care about what he or she did. Designers are cursed. Cursed with taste, and cursed with a fastidiousness about what we do. Taste is a fatal flaw to possess if you want to make money. Designers have to live with this flaw in their chromosomes. And it makes life difficult, especially in the modern world where we have to be able to pay our mortgages, our rents, our insurance premiums, our pension contributions; a world where nothing is cheap, and even less is free. It used to be possible for creative people in the 60s and 70s to live cheaply outside of the system. But Thatcher and Reagan put paid to that. Contemporary life is now a complex financial net, and poverty is not an option. Besides, who wants to end up in the clutches of the oleaginous loan companies that have colonised daytime TV; sleazy men and women telling people with financial problems that all their worries can be erased by borrowing even more money. I'd rather live on a rubbish heap in Sao Paulo than sell my soul to those people.

As designers, we have the satisfaction of doing something that we love, and which is linked directly to our own individual efforts, talent and cultural predisposition. Stop anyone in the street and ask them what they want to do with their lives and the vast majority will reply — be creative. Designers can claim this. Of course, any occupation can be creative; plumbing is creative (and more important than design). But to be paid for our ideas, to be paid for our talent, is a great privilege — even if we don't earn as much as merchant bankers. And don't ask me how much I got paid for writing this article? I'm not telling.

*   *   *

Adrian Shaughnessy is a freelance writer and art director,
and the associate creative director of This Is Real Art.
His new book, *How to be a graphic designer ... without losing your soul,*
will be published in 2005.

167

£6·48P

HAD A BARBECUE
April 1st

SATURDAY

POUNDS
PENCE

Pages 168–173
Matthew Savidge
**Findings based on an average
of £10 a day** (Excerpt)
04.2000
Self-published
148 × 210 mm, 36 pages

'While I was at college, I noticed that I would
draw at least £10 from my bank account
every day. This book is a record, of how much
money I brought home each night.'

People say that money is not foremost in life, but way ahead of whatever comes second place. It's called dough, bread, gravy, glittering filth, and the ticket to bliss. They say money talks because social contracts involve exchanges and tests of power and position. We're happy when we have more than the other guy, but are uncomfortable about holes in other people's pockets. From birth to death we struggle with gain and loss, our soul being the last remaining unpaid accountant.

Small change
Text by Jeff Rian

I live in a reasonably nice neighborhood in Paris, and just about every day I walk down the hill to the metro where I meet my beggar. He's a toothless little guy with a big smile, a graying beard, and hair the length of a page in a Lancelot comicbook. He's at least 50 but has an impish grin and a kid's glint in his eyes. His three-quarter-length coat hangs way below his knees. Except for the sneakers, he seems from another era, say, a cook named Grits in a cowboy movie starring John Wayne. I don't know what his living situation is, but he doesn't seem to drink, and he changes clothes, other than the coat, with some frequency. Since I've lived here, the past two years, I've watched him work the same section of the block nearly every day.

When he sees me he yells out, *'Ça va!'* His little hand reaches out expectantly. I give him all or most of the change in my pocket. OK, I give him up to a Euro, occasionally two. When I have nothing, poof he's gone, seeking another handout.

Walking down the hill I sometimes separate the larger from the smaller change — if I have so much; then putting them in separate pockets. I feel a twinge of guilt, thinking I should give him a real handout. Then I postpone grandiosity and imagine a big holiday handout, which, of course, never comes. I don't traipse down the hill during holidays. I'm generally gone. But so is he. And I can't imagine where.

Before living in Paris I lived for many years in Brooklyn. There, I had the same pattern of giving — usually picking one person on my familiar route to work in Manhattan. I once gave a ten-dollar bill to a windshield washer on Delancey Street. It was dark out. It must be twelve years ago. I was driving into town from my apartment in Greenpoint, Brooklyn. I thought it was a one-dollar bill that I'd torn out of my jacket pocket. But there it was: a ten. The man smiled so happily, I not only made his day, his appreciation made mine. I still remember how surprise bloomed on his face. As I recall I'd just been paid generously for something. I'm embarrassed to remember that pathetic little generosity now.

Here, I return my guy's *Ça va?* And the imp says an honest 'merci,' his right hand patting his chest as people do these days. Of course, he calibrates his thank you according to the amount given. I justify my small gift by its regularity — four or five times a week for nearly two years.

Choosing him as the recipient of my pathetic munificence allows me to deny the other beggars I run into. That's my calculation. I can imagine him growing tired of the same smallness of change. Everyone wants a raise.

Our interaction is a cheap social payoff for me. He's interested in money. I make it social by looking him in the eye and asking how he is — which is a charade. I'm never going to invite him home to take a shower. I should, but I don't want to get that close to him. What do I know about the guy? I give him change because by doing so the weight of the countless others I don't give to is reduced. That's the excuse I offer to myself. It's a busy street and there are surely more donors.

Perhaps I should mention here that the only change I have is what's in my pocket. I don't accumulate change. I cured myself of change jars years ago on the advice of a co-worker at the publishing house in Manhattan where I once worked. My friend told me to carry eleven pennies in my pocket every day and to make sure I spent those pennies. I used to have jars full of them. I followed his advice and in a few weeks I had no change in the house — and still don't. Honestly I'm happier, and certainly lighter without those jars. But it means that I don't have much change to give out. What change I accumulate today he'll get tomorrow. That's how it goes. Right now I have one euro and sixty-two cents in the right front pocket of my jeans. I'll give him the sixty-two cents and spend the euro on a coffee before I have to teach my class today. If I only have larger amounts, say only one- and two-euro coins, which is rare, I'll give him one euro, sometimes a two-euro coin.

I have a musician friend who spent twelve years panhandling on Market Street in San Francisco. He says he got by on his talent. People gave to him because he played his instrument so well (eventually he spotted by a local nightclub and has been off the streets ever since).

– – – – – – – – – – – – – – – – –

I imagine beggars have always existed, but what did they beg for before there was money?

MONDAY

POUNDS
PENCE

£13·10P

RESTED IN BED FOR WEEK AHEAD
April 9th

POUNDS
PENCE

SUNDAY

£20·33P

ARGUED WITH ÅSA
April 10th

MONDAY

£10·12P

ATE LOTS & LOTS OF FOOD
April 16th

POUNDS PENCE

SUNDAY

He also said that those without a talent of some kind often starved. That thought increases my discomfort.

I imagine beggars have always existed, but what did they beg for before there was money? Food? Fresh kill? Better rags to wear?

Money gave us a practical means to classify our power and status — the rich from poor, the Haves from the Have-Nots, the Brahmins from the outcasts. Surely if money didn't exist, our discomfort and our obligations to share would be different, if only because the symbolic value wouldn't be so starkly numerical and our material lives so different. Outcasts like my beggar test us by making us uncomfortable — their plight versus ours. His wretchedness pains me, even though, superficially, he doesn't show his suffering — which I can't figure out at all. Maybe if he were only recently on the street he'd be angrier. I would be.

Before people used money, other means of exchange were things like weighed silver, grains, cocoa beans. The Lydians invented coins in the seventh century, B.C. The Romans started minting coins in the fourth century, B.C. Mostly they were used for government purchases.

Those Lydian coins were invented about the time the Greek alphabet — the first true alphabet — directly linked speech to writing by including vowels. Both money and literacy took over the world; they were the foundations of civilization, the sources of power and control, our means of concentrating wealth and power. Wealth defined us. Labor was specialized. Now, 2700 years later, an enormous middle class supports the rich and might even be more generous to the poor. Poverty has always been bad. But being poor *and* illiterate makes things far worse.

We call money the root of evil; therefore, the invention of scoundrels. Realistically speaking, money was instrumental in freeing people from oppression. It provided a practical means to gain status. All you had to do was make it or find a way to get your hands on it. Most of us middle-classers grumble about money because we have to earn it, and to earn it we have to work, and to get a job we have to train ourselves or study something. Supposedly work makes us free. It depends on the return.

I'm middle-class according to my tax bracket. But living in this neighborhood makes me realize that middle-class costs are higher than real middle-class wages. It seems the discrepancies in purchasing power have dragged on for decades. My earning capabilities

— — — — — — — — — — — — —

… money and literacy took over the world; they were the foundations of civilization, the sources of power and control …

are only limited by my lack of ambition. I don't have the advantage of class or inheritance. My literacy has gotten me work. I live comfortably, but not extravagantly. I'm not particularly materialistic. I've moved far too often. Because of my lifestyle — freelance writer, occasional musician, nomadic until recently — and because I take public transportation all the time, I see beggars with greater frequency than, say, the rich art dealers and successful professionals I come into contact with. I'm further down the food chain. I give because 'there but for the grace of Godot, go I.' It's not just a question of guilt or empathy. Because of *my* social status I run into beggars and not-so-well-off people with greater frequency.

According to evolutionary biologists a human trait described as reciprocal altruism has been genetically bred into us. Darwin is credited with suggesting the idea that helping others helps us in return, if only by bolstering our self-image. Neo-Darwinians speak of selfish genes and how behavior is also a genetic inheritance. In *The Moral Animal* (1994), Robert Wright cites a 1971 essay by Robert Trivers, 'The Evolution of Reciprocal Altruism,' which states that 'friendship, dislike, moralistic aggression, gratitude, trust, suspicion, aspects of guilt, and some form of dishonesty and hypocrisy can be explained as important adaptations to regulate the altruistic system.' The altruistic system is the necessary niceness we often need in our social lives and encounters — even if a mask. I have to admit, when passing my beggar I've felt everything Trivers mentions, often within moments of each other. These feelings hit us during some part of every day. They arise in every social situation, and are the basis for our psychological dilemmas and our interactions. Feelings of dislike, moralistic aggression, suspicion, guilt, dishonesty and hypocrisy are strongly affected by our financial status — where we live, how we live, and what expect. I suspect my guy plays me through his mask of niceness. His mask allows me to get away with my meager generosity. It's an arrangement that is only partly conscious, for both of us. In all likelihood this semi-conscious social exchange is an acquired habit.

For that matter, morality is a social device needed by social animals — especially animals like us always watching each other and often saying it aloud — or in print. As evolutionary biologists suggest, human survival began in small groups in which everyone watched out for the other guy and in which our reputations were always at stake. Feelings of sympathy, gratitude, guilt, obligation, moral indignation, self-righteousness arise in social circumstances. We try to control them in our drive for social status. We devise laws and punishments to reign in ourselves and the other guy. Yet we exploit these emotions, as much as they seem to exploit us. And we are always calibrating their exchange value.

In the case of my guy, once we started looking each other in the eye, I could no longer avoid him. Seeing him makes me uncomfortable. Seeing him see me makes me even more uncomfortable. We've entered each other's universe, which is what he needs. The value for me is social: I perform a minor public service. I'm noticed on my street when I give some change. It's not that I want witnesses. I want to quell the discomfort that I feel. But that discomfort arose from my own ingrained social awareness.

My beggar probably doesn't have an address; therefore, he can't apply for assistance, won't find employment, doesn't wash regularly, etc. He begs. He

£2·59P

GOT SOME FREELANCE WORK
APRIL 17TH

MONDAY

£6·7P

WORKED ON DIAGRAMS
APRIL 18TH

TUESDAY

£1·19P

CONTINUED TO WORK FOR CASH
April 19th

WEDNESDAY

£5·69P

WENT SHOPPING WITH MUM
April 21st

POUNDS PENCE

FRIDAY

If money freed people from oppression it also offered all of us a means to win status …

— — — — — — — — — — — — — — —

might hide his anger to increase his take. Weak social positions force people into behavioral compromises. Maybe my guy drinks alone, and flies into terrible rages and has mentally murdered me countless times. I don't kill him in my mind, but I keep him at bay with small change.

Life's unfairness hits me when I see beggars — but not all beggars, because I protect myself by avoiding their eyes. I don't give to the gypsy girls sitting on the metro steps moaning like would-be martyrs. Theirs is an act as my reaction is a prejudice. Maybe I fool myself into thinking my guy is more deserving, and that his act is different, somehow more honest, to me. That may be because we've seen each other and have increased our social exchange rates.

I don't know if my guy can read either. I suspect he can. He might be an accountant, judging by how fast he counts coins. Nor can I really judge how different he is from me. I feel that a certain degree of literacy is a form of protection against falling through the social cracks. That's a threadbare idea I cling to out of habit. Most of us think a bit of education will protect us from the skids. With inbred expectation, call it blind hope, we think it will get us through disasters, like losing a job. So we align ourselves with a group. The group determines the kinds of social exchanges we make, and provides the semblance of a net.

Handouts are one easy device for paying status obligations. These obligations are an acquired characteristic. I pay the price my sense of status incites me to pay. My small change is tantamount to a few Hail Marys after a cheap confession, where going by the easier selection of broken commandments earned a minor penance. Confessions are cheap ways to subdue guilt. I give what I can afford, even though I feel I should give more. The feeling of responsible generosity is written into our genetic program. My guy offers me some release from an abstract social tension. I only go so far. My guy needs a shower, but I won't offer him one. I give him change, thinking he might get a shower in a shelter. He isn't always covered in filth. Sometimes I see him in completely different clothes. They look clean enough to me.

Maybe a neo-conservative fundamentalist would have a different opinion, thinking that praying for one poor sot will influence the wretch's self-delivery from

squalor — that he'll raise himself up out of penury's
deadness. I don't subscribe to such fantasies. But I can
imagine how prayer offers believers a conceptual doorway
out of social responsibility. I'm of the opinion that
thoughts don't offer much in the way of comfort, even
if the thoughts are generously conceived. And yet such
thoughts lie at the heart of our social consciousness.

Then I wonder if money doesn't provide the means
to lower the exchange value. If money freed people
from oppression it also offered all of us a means to
win status; it allowed those giving it out a symbolic
release, repaid as tokens of self-esteem and, maybe,
social recognition. People are only expected to give what
they can afford. The bottom line is the impression we
make, not the amount actually given.

My middle-class brain thinks that generosity is
inversely proportional to wealth; that people with less
money are more generous — which may not be true at all.
Maybe the richer you are, the further you are removed
from squalor. At that remove, your reputation for
generosity will be judged differently. The rich can also
benefit differently from their generosity, through tax
abatements. I'm not sure I can deduct my guy.

Cheapness, like cheating, can hurt one's
reputation. If what counts most are the impressions one
gives, one only needs to fulfill a social obligation by
seeming to be generous instead of seeming to be cheap. How
we are perceived in society counts more than how we feel
ourselves. Appearance can be calculated in relationship
to how we are watched. But other people's radar for
cheapness is often stronger than our calculated social
masks.

There are days when I want to avoid my guy.
Sometimes I don't have a cent on me, or so little that
I don't want the discomfort of his disappointment.
Sometimes I'm just tired of the whole thing. I imagine
offering him a shower, some clothes, a night in a hotel.
I don't because of the effort it would take. So I let him
have the small change, and so far it's been OK. That's
about it.

*   *   *

Jeff Rian writes about art, and other things, and plays guitar,
he lives and works in Paris.
Matthew Savidge is a graphic designer,
he lives and works in London.

173

Issue Seven—Graphic Magazine
Write+Discuss+Comment

£20·5P

EASTER DAY, ATE A LOT
APRIL 23RD

SUNDAY

£3·12P

LIKED A GIRL FROM N.Y. CITY
APRIL 28TH

FRIDAY

GRAPHIC is distributed by:

Australia
Tower Books
Unit 2, 17 Rodborough Road
Frenchs Forest, NSW 2086
T +62 2 9975 5566
F +62 2 9975 5599
E towerbks@zipworld.com.au
www.foliograph.com.au

Belgium
Bookstores
Exhibitions International
Kol. Begaultlaan 17
B-3012 Leuven
T +32 16 296 900
F +32 16 284 540
E orders@exhibitionsinternational.be
www.exhibitionsinternational.be

Other
Imapress
Brugstraat 51
B-2300 Turnhout

France
Critique Livres Distribution SAS
BP 93-24 rue Malmaison
93172 Bagnolet Cedex
T +33 1 4360 3910
F +33 1 4897 3706
E critiques.livres@wanadoo.fr

Germany
Bookstores
Sales representative South Germany:
Stefan Schempp
Augsburger Strasse 12
D-80337 München
T +49 89-230 77 737
F +49 89-230 77 738
E verlagsvertretung.schempp@t-online.de

North Germany
Sales Representative
Kurt Salchli
Marienburger Strasse 10
D-10405 Berlin
T +49 30 4171 7530
F +49 30 4171 7531
E salchli@t-online.de

Germany, Austria & Switzerland
Distribution/Auslieferung
GVA Gemeinsame Verlagsauslieferung Göttingen
Anna-Vandenhoeck-Ring 36
37081 Göttingen
Germany
T +49 551 487 177
F +49 051 413 92
E krause@gva-verlage.de

Other
IPS Pressevertrieb GmbH
Carl-Zeiss-Strasse 5
D-53340 Meckenheim
T +49 22 258801 122
F +49 22 258801 199
E publishing@ips-pressevertrieb.de
www.ips-pressevertrieb.de

Indonesia
Aksara
Jalan Kemang Raya 8b
Jakarta 12730
T +62 21 7199 288
F +62 21 7199 282
E info@aksara.com
www.aksara.com

Italy
Idea srl
Via Lago Trasimeno, 23/2 (ZI)
36015 Schio (VI)
T +39 455 576 574
F +39 445 577 764
E info@ideabooks.it
www.ideabooks.it

Red Edizioni Sas
Viale Prampolini 110
41100 Modena
T +39 59 212 792
F +39 59 4392 133
E info@redonline.it

Librimport Sas
Via Biondelli 9
20141 Milano
T +39 2 8950 1422
F +39 2 8950 2811
E librimport@libero.it

Japan
Shimada Yosho
T.Place, 5-5-25, Minami-Aoyama, Minato-Ku
Tokyo, 107-0062
T +81 3 3407 3937
F +81 3 3407 0989
E sales@shimada.attnet.ne.jp

Korea
Beatboy Inc.
Kangnam-Ku Shinsa-Dong 666-11
Baegang Building 135-897
Seoul
T +82 2 3444 8367
F +82 2 541 8358
E yourbeatboy@hanmail.net

Malaysia
How & Why Sdn Bhd
101A, Jalan SS2/24
47300 Petaling Jaya
Selangor
T +60 3 7877 4800
F +60 3 7877 4600
E info@howwwhy.com
www.howwwhy.com

Mexico
LHR Distribuidor de Libros
Calle 11 No. 69-1
Col.V. Gomez Farias Mexico
D.F. 15010 Mexico
T +52 55 5785 8996
F +52 55 5785 7816
E lhrlibro@prodigy.net.mx
www.lhrlibros.com

The Netherlands
Bookstores
Betapress BV
Burg. Krollaan 14
5126 PT Gilze
T +31 161 457 800
F +31 161 457 224

Other
BIS Publishers
Herengracht 370-372
1016 CH Amsterdam
T +31 20 524 7560
F +31 20 524 7557
E bis@bispublishers.nl
www.bispublishers.nl

Russia
Design Books
3 Maly Kislovsky Lane office 315
Moscow 103009
T +7 095 203 65 94
F +7 095 203 65 94

Scandinavia
(Denmark, Finland, Norway, Sweden)
Sales Representative
Bo Rudin
Box 5058
SE-165 11 Hasselby
Sweden
T +46 8 894 080
F +46 8 388 320
E b.m@rudins.com

Singapore
Basheer Graphic Books
Block 231, Bain Street
#04–19 Bras Basah Complex
180231 Singapore
T +65 336 0810
F +65 334 1950

Page One Pte Ltd
20 Kaki Bukit View
Kaki Bukit Techpark II
415956 Singapore
T +65 744 2088
F +65 744 2088
E pageone@singnet.com.sg

Spain
ACTAR
Roca i Batlle 2 i 4
08023 Barcelona
T +34 93 418 77 59
F +34 93 418 67 07
E info@actar-mail.com
www.actar.es

Taiwan
Long Sea International Book Co.,Ltd.
1/F No. 204 Si Wei Rd
Taipei 106 Taiwan ROC
T +886 2 2706 6838
F +886 2 2706 6109
E thfang@ms16.hinet.net
www.longsea.co.tw

Turkey
Evrensel Grafikir Yayincilik
Gulbahar Mahl
Gayret SK No:11
80300-01 Mecidiyekoy/Istanbul
T +90 212 356 7276
F +90 212 356 7278
E evrensely@superonline.com

United Kingdom
Bookstores
Airlift Book Company
8 The Arena
Mollison Avenue
Enfield, Middlesex EN3 7NL
T +44 20 8804 0400
F +44 20 8804 0044
E info@airlift.co.uk
www.airlift.co.uk

Other
Comag Specialist
Tavistock Works
Tavistock Road
West Drayton
Middlesex UB7 7QX
T +44 1895 433 800
F +44 1895 433 801
E andy.hounslow@comag.co.uk

USA/Canada
Lords News International
133 Jefferson Avenue
Jersey City, NJ 07306
T +1 201 798 2555
F +1 201 798 5335
lordnewsinc@hotmail.com
www.lordsusa.com

USA/West Coast
Trucatriche
3800 Main Street Suite 8
Chula Vista, CA 91911
California
T +1 619 426 2690
F +1 619 426 2695
E info@trucatriche.com

Subscriptions to graphic
(all prices include airmail)

1 year (4 issues)
○ Europe EUR80/GBP55
○ USA/Canada USD105
○ Other countries USD125

2 years (8 issues)
○ Europe EUR149/GBP103
○ USA/Canada USD195
○ Other countries USD225

Students
(valid only with a copy of your student
registration form)

1 year (4 issues)
○ Europe EUR63/GBP43.50
○ USA/Canada USD90
○ Other countries USD100

Fax this form to:
+31 20 524 75 57

or send to:
graphic
Herengracht 370–372
1016 CH Amsterdam
The Netherlands

code GR/BZ/07

Payment (for prompt delivery please pay by credit card)
○ Please charge my: ○ Visa ○ AmEx ○ Euro/Master
○ Please invoice me/my company
(first issue will be sent on receipt of payment)

Mr/Ms   Name _____   Surname _____

Card number _____   CVC–2 Code * _____

Expiry date _____   Signature _____

Company _____

Address ** _____

City _____   Postcode/Zip _____

Country _____   Telephone _____

Email _____   Fax _____

*: Please add your CVC–2 code (the last 3 digits of the number printed
on the signature strip on the back of your card) if paying by Mastercard.

**: Please also attach details of card billing address if different from delivery address.

Cover printed on
250 g/m² Luxocard I

SCHNEIDER

PAPIER

papergrades used in this issue are
ted out of the international collection
hneider Papier...

nore information:
v.schneider-papier.nl
al 0031 30 6629222

PEOPLE AND PAPER

Yie Chien Wu

Translated by Darren Buckingham

Y IE CHIEN WU was an only child from a poor family in Pang Ho. His clothes were scant and his shoes worn to threads as fine as butterflies wings. Different from the other boys and their families, he sat a forlorn figure at the back of class, alone with his indifference. Often taunted and bullied, Yie Chien Wu sought solace and comfort away from the glare of ignorance and intolerance under the shade of his favourite wanga tree. Feeding from his meagre provisions, Yie Chien Wu would sit and watch those around him gorge on racks of lamb and revel in their asparagus sprigs and minted dips.

Yie Chien Wu was of pure heart and innocence; his virtue overflowed in abundance. Each night before slumber heavied, Yie Chien Wu would pray to the Four Directional Winds of Good Fortune to blow his way and rid him and his family of their lot.

One day after school, wallowing in his thoughts and wishes, he strayed from the path back to Pang Ho and found himself lost in the Forgotten Forest of Potential Futures. Mist began to settle. Cold and frightened, he followed a dimly lit opening towards the stream. In the distance, the figure of an old man fishing at the brook came into view. As Yie Chien Wu got closer he could see that his robes were of the finest silk and his hair was as wild as that of an ox.

'Your name is Yie Chien Wu,' said the old man. 'How do you know my name?' replied Yie Chien Wu. 'The Celestial Ancestors had spoken of a day when a young boy with pure heart but heavy mind would come seeking elevation from his woes and the answers to life's injustices.' 'It's true, old man,' replied Yie Chien Wu. 'I long to be the same as the other boys and their families.' 'You long to be like the others, with their shoes made of goat and their stomachs full of flesh. You believe these things will grant you happiness?', asked the old man.

'Those of which you speak are happy only in their foolish misguidedness. Their happiness is one derived and driven by delusion. If you attain and value these things above all else in the belief it will bring you and your family happiness, your heart will be tainted and your path to true enlightenment will be wayward and fraught with obstacles. This is not the way. It is written by the Great Sages that some people will find satisfaction in good food and fine clothes, money and status. When these objects are attained they are not satisfied. It is better to remain silent and truthful to oneself, not being bound by custom and social convention. Let yourself grow naturally. Your mode of living has its own place in the universe. If you try and change your way of life, you will upset the balance of things and the order of the universe

will be disturbed. All things have their place in the universe. They fulfil their function in simply being what they are. You are Yie Chien Wu. If you take this wisdom and gain understanding from it, your path to attainment will be natural and unhindered. If you do not, calamity will follow and you will forever be lost.'

In an instant, the mist of the forest swirled and entwined Yie Chien Wu until his vision was obscured in a heavy white cloud of blindness. Then suddenly, as quickly as the mist had descended, it vanished. Yie Chien Wu now found himself standing at the door of his parents' house in Pang Ho.

That night, having listened to the words of the old man, Yie Chien Wu began to sew himself a costume and set sail for the Land of Plenty, where he would try his luck as a WWE wrestler.

On his raft made of pinecones and sugar twine, Yie Chien Wu crossed the treacherous Sea of Misforgiving. Six days passed and the Land of Plenty neared the horizon. As Yie Chien Wu approached, he could see that waiting upon the shore was a chauffeur-driven limousine. It was as sleek as any chariot he had ever seen. It stood proudly before him glistening like a freshly opened tin of peach halves. Yie Chien Wu clambered inside and was taken aback by the luxuriousness of the tanned leather furnishings. The limousine was to carry Yie Chien Wu to the bright lights of the big city where an appearance on the Tonight Show with Jay Leno beckoned. Yie Chien Wu stood anxiously in the wings as the big announcement was made: 'From Pang Ho! Ladies and Gentlemen! Yie Chien Wu!' The rousing reception that greeted Yie Chien Wu overwhelmed him with feelings of popularity and immense significance. The captive audience listened with eager ears and baited breath, as Yie Chien Wu impressed them with his newfound confidence and enthusiasm for wealth and success.

Overnight, Yie Chien Wu had become the talk of the town. Money and status quickly followed. This filled Yie Chien Wu with a sense of brighter and greater tomorrows. Yie Chien Wu began

shopping at Bloomingdale's and receiving invites to the most expensive and exclusive restaurants in the city, socialising with people of great importance and notability such as Danny DeVito and Cissy Spacek. But Yie Chien Wu was beginning to tread a delicate path in the expensive Italian shoes that now adorned his feet.

The following morning was the day of Yie Chien Wu's fight. His challenge was against one of the lands mightiest warriors: 'The Block'. That evening, multitudes gathered from far and wide. The arena seethed and bubbled with excited anticipation. 'Yie Chien Wu!' – 'Yie Chien Wu!', they cried. The bell rang out and Yie Chien Wu moved cautiously towards his opponent, like a cat on roller skates. The Block, quick to attack, put Yie Chien Wu in a crippling broadside-camel clutch followed by a devastating reverse angled monkey check off the ropes. Yie Chien Wu was killed.

A week passed and Yie Chien Wu's family received news of their son's death back in Pang Ho. The pair of expensive Italian shoes Yie Chien Wu had worn with such pride and joy during his short spell in WWE were passed on to his father, but were of no use – he had just lost both his feet that afternoon in a wheat-sheafing accident.

Many generations passed, and the memory of Yie Chien Wu began to fade, the remnants of his tale existing solely as a late night fable. The villagers of Pang Ho would often speak of a distant forest where a young boy with potential, pure heart and innocence once entered, seeking elevation from his woes and the answers to life's injustices, but never returned. Many people since had found and entered the forest. Some returned; others did not. Those that did return told of seeing a pair of expensive Italian leatherwares near a brook. The likes of which, they never really attached much importance to.

THE END